D0899648

REMARKABLE
WOMEN
of
Old Lyme

JIM LAMPOS & MICHAELLE PEARSON

THE
History
PRESS

Published by The History Press
Charleston, SC 29403
www.historypress.net

First published 2015

Manufactured in the United States

ISBN 978.1.62619.790.9

Library of Congress Control Number: 2015933529

To Phoebe and Silvanos, with love.

Contents

CONTENTS

Acknowledgements

The authors wish to thank the following organizations and people for their assistance in making *Remarkable Women of Old Lyme* possible.

Connecticut Historical Society
Connecticut State Library
Florence Griswold Museum
Lyme Academy College of Fine Arts
Museum of Connecticut History
New London Library
Old Lyme Historical Society
Old Lyme Phoebe Griffin Noyes Library

Nicole Wholean for her assistance at the Lyme Historical Society Archive.
Alison Mitchell for her support and suggestions.
C. Townsend Ludington for his insights and editorial advice.
Mary Fiorelli, Linda Alexander and the entire staff at the OLPGN Library, for everything.
Sierra Dixon and the staff of the Connecticut Historical Society.
Diana Atwood-Johnson, Christopher B. Steiner and Whitney Talcott for their insights and assistance with images.
Jennifer Hillhouse, Ned Perkins, Jim Meehan and William Eastman for providing images when we needed them most.
Kathryn Winchell and Judy Tooker for ideas and introductions.
A special thank-you to Robert Couteau for his sage advice and editing.

Founders and Revolutionaries

An Introduction to Old Lyme

S ituated on the Connecticut coast, about halfway between New York and Boston, the town of Old Lyme* is not your typical suburban community. From its founding, this venerable town has prided itself on being quirky and independent. Its rich history is written on the landscape and cherished in the hearts of its citizens. A great many of the heroic figures who have shaped Old Lyme's history and character are women. Some of their stories are well known and often retold while others have unjustly been forgotten. The purpose of this book will be to recollect the old stories, uncover new ones and celebrate the accomplishments of these women who deserve to be remembered by future generations.

The women of Old Lyme have been pioneers in politics, business, education and the arts. Perhaps the unique circumstances of the town's settlement encouraged a strong streak of self-reliance and creativity in these women.

Old Lyme was part of the Saybrook Colony, and unlike neighboring colonies, such as Massachusetts Bay and Rhode Island, Saybrook was not founded as a religious refuge. It was founded in 1635 by the followers of Oliver Cromwell, the "parliamentarians" of the English Civil War, who sought to dethrone King Charles I and establish a more representative English government. They were landed gentry, entrepreneurs and investors—a class that was ascendant in terms of influence and power in the early seventeenth

---

*. After the "Loving Parting," what is now Old Lyme was called Lyme, which encompassed today's Lyme, Old Lyme, East Lyme and part of Salem. Though Lyme and Old Lyme separated in 1855, people continued to use "Lyme" for both well into the mid-twentieth century.

century. They established Saybrook Colony at the mouth of the Connecticut River primarily for commercial purposes and also as a place of refuge for Cromwellian "gentlemen of quality" should they need to flee England and establish a government-in-exile. Unlike the surrounding colonies founded by religious dissenters who were nevertheless loyal to the Crown, Saybrook's founders were enemies to the king.

Once Cromwell's victory seemed assured, Saybrook was no longer needed as a place of refuge. Governor George Fenwick sold Saybrook Colony to the Colony of Connecticut in 1644 and returned to England the following year to fight alongside Cromwell's forces. He then was appointed commissioner to the trial of King Charles I. The king was charged with treason, found guilty and beheaded in 1649.

Fenwick bequeathed the colony's land east of the Connecticut River to Matthew Griswold in 1645. Making his home at the confluence of the Black Hall and Connecticut Rivers along the shores of the Long Island Sound, Griswold was the first settler of what would become Old Lyme. The lands of the former Saybrook Colony were now in the hands of gentlemen farmers, ship's captains, tradesmen, artisans and men like Griswold who were primarily concerned with securing their own prosperity. These were practical people who were not hidebound by religious convention or custom. They relied on their wives to administer their affairs and manage their estates while they were away at sea or tending to other business, and from the earliest records, we find something unique: property owned by women in their own names.

It was not only unusual for married women to hold property in their own names but also practically unheard of, even illegal. But Old Lyme was not a usual sort of place. The Salisbury-MacCurdy *Family Histories and Genealogies* notes that "in Connecticut as everywhere else in New England, the property of a wife, unless it was settled upon her before marriage, went by law to the husband, subject to his disposal." Matthew Griswold, however, "had a liberal and enlarged view, very much in advance of his age." Hannah Griswold inherited substantial meadowlands in Windsor, Connecticut, while she was married to Matthew. In a document dated April 23, 1663, it was written that "this parcel of meadow is allowed by her Husband Matthew Griswold to be recorded and made over to Hannah his wife to remain to her and her children, and their Dispose, forever." It would be a mistake to make too much of this fact and say that women enjoyed equal station with men in seventeenth-century Old Lyme, but still, we can say that by virtue of their administration of family estates and direct ownership of land, these women had an authority and economic empowerment that was unusual and quite possibly unique for the time.

Along with this measure of women's economic empowerment, the second unique factor in Old Lyme was its attitude toward religion. Not only civic custom but also religious law proscribed the role of women. While no doubt devout, Old Lyme's residents seemed to adopt a more cavalier attitude toward religious matters than the typical New Englander. When Old Lyme, then called Lyme, separated from Saybrook in 1665 (an event known as the "Loving Parting") and established itself as an independent town, Moses Noyes was hired to be the new town's preacher. Noyes would not become a regularly ordained minister, however, and Lyme would not formally organize a church until nearly thirty years later, in 1693.

In *Lyme Miscellany 1776–1976*, Christopher Collier writes:

> *Thus the secular dominance manifested in Lyme's history is intrinsic to its records. Without an approved church, Moses Noyes was not ordained and was therefore officially unable to administer the sacraments of baptism*

The 1660 Thomas Lee House, where Reinold Marvin courted Phoebe Lee. *Photograph by M. Pearson.*

and communion. Subsequent events indicated that they continued without religious organization until 1693. This was certainly a most extraordinary lack of godly concern for seventeenth century Connecticut. Indeed, this anomalous situation may have been unique.

Perhaps it was this early irreverence that gave the women of Lyme a little bit of breathing room and allowed them to have something else that seems to be unique for the day: a wicked good sense of humor.

It is hardly possible to read a local history of Old Lyme and not encounter certain oft-told tales of its early women. Indeed, these stories are woven into the very fabric of the town's history. We often hear the tale of the lovely, demure Phoebe Lee, born on August 14, 1677, at the Lee House, a homestead built by her father in 1660 in what is now East Lyme. One day, when nineteen-year-old Phoebe was attending to her chores, her suitor, Captain Reinold Marvin, rode up to the Lee House on his horse (using a sheepskin instead of a saddle as protest against paying certain church tithes) and announced to her that

the Lord had commanded they be married. Phoebe demurely replied, "The Lord's Will be Done." Whether it was the Lord's will or not, Phoebe's father did not favor the union. It was the law then to post intentions of marriage in a public place. Captain Marvin caused a bit of a stir, as his announcement read, "Reinold Marvin and Phoebe Lee, Do intend to marry. Though her dad opposed be, They can no longer tarry."

The captain and Phoebe did indeed marry in 1696

Grave of Phoebe Lee Marvin at Duck River Cemetery. *Authors' collection.*

and had five children. After Phoebe died on October 27, 1707, Reinold Marvin returned to the Lees the lands that Phoebe had inherited during their marriage, perhaps as a demonstration to Phoebe's family that he had married her for love and not money.

The doings of Ursula Wolcott can hardly be avoided when reading early histories. Born in Windsor, Connecticut, on October 30, 1724, Ursula was the daughter of Governor Roger Wolcott and described as a woman of "great beauty, energy, and amiability." Ursula decided to marry her cousin Matthew Griswold of Old Lyme. On her visits to Black Hall, she would flirt with her taciturn cousin whenever she passed him in the hall or on the stairs, asking, "What did you say, Cousin Matthew?" Matthew would reply, "Nothing" and go on his sullen way. Round and round they went with this charade until one day Matthew offered his usual rebuff, "Nothing," to her question of "What did you say?" Ursula retorted, "Well, it's time that you did!" After this breaking of the ice, Matthew Griswold and Ursula Wolcott were married on November 10, 1743, further cementing the bonds between two of Connecticut's most powerful founding families. Ursula was a most able and amiable consort to Matthew, who became governor of Connecticut and a dedicated patriot of the American Revolution.

On one occasion, with the British fleet anchored just offshore from his home, soldiers raided Griswold's estate with orders to seize the Revolutionary governor. Seeing what was about to happen, Ursula quickly hid Matthew inside a large meat barrel. When the soldiers came to the house, the charming Ursula graciously invited them inside to inspect the house and the grounds and calmly offered them tea. She told the soldiers that her husband was well on his way to Hartford to attend a meeting of the legislature. Satisfied, the soldiers left, and Matthew safely emerged from the barrel.

On another occasion, Matthew was being pursued by British soldiers up Whippoorwill Road. When he reached the Marvin House with the soldiers in hot pursuit, young Hetty Marvin was laying homespun linen on the grass to bleach. Quick-thinking Hetty told the governor to dive under the linen, and when the soldiers arrived and asked if Griswold had passed that way, she quite honestly answered, "No, he did not pass." The soldiers turned back, and Governor Griswold emerged and continued on his way.

Some of the most entertaining stories to emerge from this period concern Governor Griswold's sister Phoebe Griswold Parsons. She is often associated with the "Black Hall Boys," or the "Pleiades," high-spirited Griswold sisters celebrated for their beauty and charisma. Athletic, independent and willful,

The Black Hall section of Old Lyme, circa 1906. *Jennifer Hillhouse collection.*

these women of Black Hall were a lyrical refrain that underscores Old Lyme's historical charm.

Phoebe Griswold was born on April 22, 1716, to Judge John and Hannah Lee Griswold. On December 14, 1731, she married Jonathan Parsons, a reverend of the Congregational Church who had a penchant for radical theology and an elegant wardrobe. Parsons was a firebrand preacher and an acolyte of Great Awakening minister Jonathan Edwards, and on March 29, 1741, he delivered a sermon affirming his rebirth and zealous affiliation with the new religious movement that was sweeping through New England. He invited the itinerant revivalist preacher George Whitefield to address his Old Lyme congregation during the height of the Great Awakening. On August 12, 1745, Whitefield gave an electrifying sermon standing atop a glacial erratic in Parsons's backyard, a boulder hence known as the Whitefield Rock, and there irrevocably split the Congregational Church in two between the revivalist "New Lights" and the traditionalist "Old Lights." Reverend Parsons's wife, Phoebe, was a new light of a different order.

Renowned for her beauty and devilish humor, Phoebe Griswold Parsons was a dedicated wife who nevertheless liked to occasionally tweak her dandy of a husband. One day, while Reverend Jonathan was preening in the mirror before a service—combing his hair and adjusting his ruffled shirt and coat trimmed with gold and silver lace—Phoebe came up behind him and, throwing her arms around his neck, kissed him and passed her hands over his face. When Parsons ascended the podium to address the congregation, he was met with giggles and puzzled stares. Little did he know that the true purpose of Phoebe's amorous gesture was to blacken his face with soot. And so, looking like an early Al Jolson, he stood before his flock and delivered his sermon. On another occasion, Jonathan was working on a difficult sermon and rehearsing his lines aloud. Just before he left, Phoebe casually picked up his text and thumbed through it. This was not unusual, as she often edited her husband's sermons and legend says that she wrote many of them herself. In this instance, however, the editing was a bit more drastic—she surreptitiously removed a page while his back was turned. Parsons ascended to the pulpit, but when he reached the climactic portion of his address, he stopped short, flustered and bewildered. The congregation murmured as its minister seemed to have completely lost his train of thought. Looking up, Reverend Parsons saw his beloved wife, Phoebe, in the front pew, smiling sweetly, fanning herself with the missing page.

These tales of Reverend Parsons and his irreverent wife are oft-repeated as entertaining anecdotes, but the significance of their words and deeds resonates in ways profoundly important not only to the history of Old Lyme but also to the American Revolution itself.

In 1766, the New Lights of Parsons's church became Old Lyme's Sons of Liberty. Phoebe and Jonathan's son Samuel Holden Parsons was an officer in the Revolutionary army, and their other son, Marshfield Parsons, converted their home on the town green into the Parsons Tavern. The tavern was a hotbed of Revolutionary fervor, hosting meetings of the Sons of Liberty, and in 1778, the Marquis de Lafayette camped his troops in front on the town green. Called the "Hero of Two Worlds," the Marquis de Lafayette served as the youngest general in the Continental army, commanding troops that would fight decisive battles in the Revolution. He returned to Old Lyme again in 1824, revisiting the tavern and spending the night at the McCurdy House across the street, where he had also stayed in 1778.

Located at the heart of Old Lyme, where the road into town curves past today's Congregational Church, the Parsons Tavern played a central role in Old Lyme's history through the coming decades and, indeed, provides a handy geographical reference point for the lives of many women profiled in this book. It was here that artist and educator Phoebe Griffin Noyes established her school and suffragist Katharine Ludington was raised.

Across the street was the home of patriot John McCurdy, where philanthropist Evelyn MacCurdy lived. Just one street away is Duck River

The Parsons Tavern. *Ludington-Saltus Records.*

Lane, where Ella Grasso, the first woman to be elected governor, made her home. Part of Parsons Tavern still stands today, but it was moved to 13 McCurdy Road in 1893 by Charles Ludington and replaced with the elegant mansion next to the church. It was in this home that Katharine Ludington lived for the rest of her life and hosted legendary parties for the nation's leading intellectuals, including medical pioneer Dr. Alice Hamilton. It was also in this home that 1929's original "girl gone wild" Josephine Noyes Rotch held her wedding party. Tragically, six months later, her funeral was held there as well.

So, it seems fitting that we begin our story here, at the bend where McCurdy Road meets Lyme Street, by the Congregational Church, before Old Lyme's historic Town Green.

Phoebe Griffin Lord Noyes

Artist and Educator

Phoebe Griffin Lord Noyes was born on February 20, 1797, at the Lord homestead on Lyme Street, located at the present site of the library that bears her name. The Lords were a prominent family who traced their roots to the founding settlers of the original Saybrook Colony. Phoebe was named for her mother, Phebe* Griffin of East Haddam. Her father, Joseph Lord, was a gentleman farmer with nearly two hundred acres of land.

After her husband's death in 1812, Phebe Lord took over management of the farm and also saw to the task of educating her daughters. Having come from a family that valued education, Lord firmly believed in the virtue of educating girls. She and her daughter Phoebe were members of the "Female Reading Society," which met every Wednesday for the purpose of "reading from the holy scriptures and any other book whose tendency is to elevate the mind and improve the heart."

As a young woman, Phebe Lord had been afforded a unique opportunity to study with her brothers, Edward and George, as they prepared for the Yale entrance exam. George later became a successful lawyer in New York and offered to educate one of his sister's children. When young Phoebe turned fourteen, her mother sent her to New York, where she resided at her uncle's home for the next several years, returning to Old Lyme each summer.

---

*. Phebe Lord used the plainer spelling of her name while her daughter chose the more sophisticated "Phoebe." The register of the Female Reading Society shows the signatures of the two women as "Phebe Lord" and "Phoebe G. Lord."

Phoebe had shown considerable artistic talent even as a child, when she painted pictures using the juices of crushed flowers and leaves for color. While in New York City, she immersed herself in her studies, paying particular attention to her French and learning the painstaking techniques of old-fashioned miniature painting from the highly regarded miniaturist Madame Vaillant. Around the same time, Phoebe's cousin William Jewett was an associate member of the prestigious National Academy of Design. It is likely that he visited George Griffin's home and may have further influenced Phoebe's artistic development.

An 1812 letter from George Griffin to Phebe Lord says, "We are very pleased with Phebe [*sic*]. Her progress in painting is very rapid." He goes on to explain that "embroidery is not a fashionable accomplishment in this city" and asks his sister to decide if it is worth the additional expense for Phoebe to pursue it, based on "what you think will be most useful to her in Connecticut."

While in her uncle's care, Phoebe also had many opportunities to refine her social graces. The *Noyes-Gilman Ancestry* says Phoebe was "very handsome, with light hair, beautiful gray eyes, fair skin, and rosy cheeks…full of fun, fond of society, and had a number of admirers."

Phoebe's letters from New York to her sisters contained practical observations of daily life and descriptions of people and places, revealing a keen eye and a sharp mind. She described the latest fashions in minute detail, often including small sketches to embellish her narrative.

When her New York sojourn ended, Phoebe returned to her home in Lyme and began teaching.

She married Daniel Noyes on May 16, 1827, at the Congregational Church after a romance that began with longing looks exchanged between Phoebe's window and the general store across the street, where Daniel was a partner.

Phoebe Griffin Noyes. *Ludington-Saltus Records.*

18

Phoebe Griffin Noyes's portrait of her children. *Ludington-Saltus Records.*

The couple initially lived in a house near Dr. Richard Noyes on Lyme Street but prepared to move as Daniel searched for business opportunities in New York or Ohio. In 1831, they decided to remain in Lyme, purchasing the house that had been the Parsons Tavern, a famous meeting place during the Revolution. In 1838, Daniel opened a store across the street, on a corner of Stephen Peck's garden, but due to various economic and social factors, his business struggled.

Around this time, Phoebe resumed her teaching career. This was considered a noble and appropriate way for a woman to contribute to the family purse, but we also hear of "her intense desire to make the most of her life by stimulating and encouraging, intellectually and morally, the many who might thus be brought under her influence."

Daniel expanded the front of the house for use as a schoolroom, and in addition to providing instruction in the fundamental subjects, Phoebe taught her students how to paint and draw.

Josephine Noyes, depicted as "Little Red Riding Hood" by her mother, Phoebe Griffin Noyes. *Ludington-Saltus Records.*

Evelyn MacCurdy Salisbury writes of Phoebe in *Family Histories and Genealogies*:

> *She taught two generations, and her high moral influence, in a constantly widening sphere, during her lifetime and since, cannot be estimated. She had one of the first art schools in this country, painting beautifully herself in water colors. She found time to paint a great many finely executed miniatures on ivory, and to teach drawing and water color painting, in addition to the usual studies, to all the girls who were under her instruction. To her influence and art teachings are due much of the refinement and elegance of living which have so remarkably distinguished the society of Lyme.*

Phoebe's unfailing moral compass was tempered by a liveliness and sense of fun that she retained throughout her life. The Noyes home was a center of activity and social life for the young people of the town. Phoebe enjoyed dancing and card playing, both of which were looked down upon by some of the more staid citizens of the town, one of whom actually prayed out loud that she might see "the error of her ways," though somehow, she never did. Instead, she advocated for the "refining influence" of dancing upon the young and often joined in a lively Virginia Reel with Daniel at the end of a social evening.

Her granddaughter Katharine Ludington writes in *Lyme-and Our Family*: "She loved young people, and loved to have them around her, and was conscious of her power over them. Her many cares never made her dull, and she was always ready, no matter how tired she was, to enter into the spirit of their frolics and amusements. She assisted in tableaux, concerts, charades, and games of all sorts."

In her later years, Phoebe remained a strong and beneficent influence on the young people of the town. She died on October 12, 1875, and is buried in the Duck River Cemetery, but her truest monument is the library that was given in her memory.

Old Lyme Phoebe Griffin Noyes Library, 2014. *Photograph by M. Pearson.*

The reading room at the Phoebe Griffin Noyes Library, circa 1898. *Old Lyme Phoebe Griffin Noyes Library Permanent Collection.*

The Old Lyme Phoebe Griffin Noyes Library was built on the site of the Lord homestead, where Phoebe was born and lived with her mother and sisters. Dedicated in 1898, the library was the gift of Josephine Noyes Ludington and Charles H. Ludington, Phoebe's daughter and son-in-law.

To this day, Phoebe's love of learning and good company is honored at the library, and her portrait hangs in a place of honor above the fireplace in the Reading Room.

2

Evelyn MacCurdy Salisbury

Writer and Philanthropist

Cousin Evelyn! Who can really put her on paper? She was so much a part of Lyme and our lives, a personality of such flavor and distinction, that her death, when she was over ninety, seemed almost incredible.
—*Katharine Ludington,* Lyme-and Our Family, *1928.*

Evelyn MacCurdy was indeed larger than life. A formidable, elegant woman known for her strong convictions, Evelyn never stopped trying to "improve" Old Lyme and its citizenry. Some of the citizens did not take so kindly to the notion of being improved, but that never bothered Evelyn. She knew what she wanted and what the town needed: a school of higher learning, a library and better educational opportunities for promising students. Family papers speak of her generosity toward impoverished but hardworking scholars and of her devotion, passion and drive regarding issues she felt strongly about.

There has been much written about Evelyn. Her intelligence, quick wit and exceptional good taste are all detailed in the histories of Old Lyme. But beneath the layers of Victorian propriety, Evelyn was a very complex and interesting person—a woman truly ahead of her time.

She was born on November 3, 1823, to Charles Johnson McCurdy[*] and Sarah Ann Lord. Her mother had a strong influence over young

---

[*]. There are many variants of McCurdy. The family's first ancestor in America was the Revolutionary War patriot John McCurdy, described as "an Irish gentleman of Scottish background." He and his descendants generally spelled the name McCurdy, but Evelyn used "MacCurdy" throughout her life.

This circa 1850 portrait of Evelyn MacCurdy Salisbury hangs in the reading room at the library. *Old Lyme Phoebe Griffin Noyes Library Permanent Collection.*

Evelyn's character. Sarah was noted for her skills as a watercolorist and also for her innate sense of gentility and generosity. She was, by all accounts, a kind and loving mother who sadly died of consumption at age thirty-five, when Evelyn was just eleven years old. Her husband, Charles, keenly felt the loss and was determined that he and Evelyn would "live for each other." This promise he kept, and they became each other's trusted friend and companion.

Evelyn was taught by Phoebe Griffin Noyes, who was like a second mother to her. Later, she traveled to New York, studying alongside her cousins at Mrs. Okill's School. She then came back to New London and New Haven to complete her education. At age eighteen, she returned to her father's house and took charge of his domestic affairs. He took Evelyn with him when traveling to Hartford, New Haven and beyond and introduced her to his circle of friends and political acquaintances. He shared his political and intellectual interests with her and "made her conversant with his legal affairs."

Charles J. McCurdy accepted the positions of judge of the Superior Court and later the Supreme Court of Connecticut. In 1851, he was asked to serve as the U.S. Chargé d'Affaires in Vienna. Naturally, he asked Evelyn to accompany him. Her accounts of their time abroad are filled with detailed observances of the protocols, manners and appearances of the "crowned heads of Europe" and their ministers, courtiers and ladies.

She was presented to Queen Victoria at a "drawing-room" and, undaunted by the pageantry and grandeur, observed, "The Queen, in blue and white brocade, was already stout for her five feet of stature; her face was not winning, but it was one which in private life would be respected and trusted."

The McCurdys were invited to enjoy the pleasures of the London season; however, Charles was anxious to report to his post in Vienna, so their engagements were limited. Nonetheless, Evelyn recorded her observations with a touch of Yankee pride, saying of the noble crowd, "To an American eye, the ladies were generally too large-boned, thin and angular, large featured, and lacking mobility and brightness of expression in youth, and too stout a figure and often flushed in complexion in maturer years, contrasted with the smoother-limbed, more flexible-featured and 'spirituelle' looking American women of all ages."

When they arrived in Vienna, it became obvious that Evelyn was lacking the European affectation of a "duenna," or chaperone to accompany her. This was made to seem slightly embarrassing, but the McCurdys stuck to the American fashion, wherein a lady traveling with her father was deemed to have sufficient protection of her character and reputation. However, this made Lady Westmoreland (the English ambassador's wife) uncomfortable, and she "showed much kindness to the young American," accompanying Evelyn whenever possible.

When Judge McCurdy's term in Vienna was over, he and Evelyn returned to their house in Old Lyme (now known as the Sill House), bringing carpets, wallpaper, artwork and other luxury items from Europe to make it "one of the few houses in the country in which harmonies and contrasts of color

The circa 1700 McCurdy House, 2014. *Photograph by M. Pearson.*

were carefully studied in furnishings and decoration…in advance of the general taste."

After the death of his father in 1860, Judge McCurdy sold the house and moved into the ancestral McCurdy manse at what is now 1 Lyme Street.

In November 1871, Evelyn married Edward Elbridge Salisbury, a professor of Sanskrit and Arabic at Yale. Their letters show great affection and respect for each other. Together they published an exhaustively researched multivolume set of family histories and genealogies, which remain an authoritative source for scholars today. In the midst of these copious family histories, Edward included a tribute to Evelyn:

> *Gifted by nature with quickness of discernment, great intelligence and a power of grasping truth firmly, she is at the same time tenderly sensitive… Her temperament is very joyous; her disposition most amiable. Even strangers have learnt that her heart is ever open to all human joys and sorrows….Nor does the failure of others to appreciate, or recognize, her generous kindness, chill the feeling in her bosom— rather does it intensify it.*

According to the *New England Historical and Genealogical Register*, Evelyn wrote for the *New York Independent* in its earlier years, under the pseudonym "Ernest," and also wrote for the *New York Tribune* and Connecticut papers. A playful missive she sent to her father dated April 10, 1889, directs his attention to two "particularly well written articles" in the *Sound Breeze* newspaper and says, "Lyme is really stirring with its fresh *Breeze*. It has really done good, and I think will do more, if it is only in waking up some hope and faith in regard for the town. People have only scoffed at any suggestion of progress. Nobody seems to look back and see any improvement there has been in the memory of man, though there has not been much growth." From the context of this letter, and her involvement with other journalistic ventures, it is very likely that Evelyn had a hand in this local newspaper. She was certainly all about progress. She regularly used a typewriter for correspondence by 1889, the first year that a lightweight portable typewriter became available, and the Salisburys were among the first to have telephone service installed at their home in New Haven around 1878.

Katharine Ludington described Evelyn in her middle age and later life as strongly resembling "Queen Victoria and whether consciously or not, [she] dressed the part to perfection…Her voice was clear, rather high, and her enunciation crisp. She always made her points carry and she never hesitated to be pointed. She had a command of forceful English—

Main Street, Old Lyme, circa 1915. *Authors' collection.*

entirely unmodernized. She rounded her sentences and used no short cuts but she never was ponderous!" "She would speak her mind to you, and then say—"Well, I have told you what I think—if you don't believe me, I wash my hands of you!"

Judge McCurdy died in December 1891, and in his will, he left Evelyn the bulk of his remaining property (after some charitable bequests), stating that he had "entire confidence in her judgment and kindness" and "I hope…she will make liberal provision for educational and other beneficent public objects in the town where I have passed my life and which I have loved so well."

Evelyn had always been interested in the subject of education, and her writings are filled with her ideas and proposals for the town. In 1885, the Old Lyme Academy, on the corner of Lyme Street and Academy Lane, burned down, and the site languished for several years due to lack of funds and disagreement among its trustees as to how to proceed. It was also suggested that the town might build a high school, and interest in the project grew. In 1893, it was reported in the *Sound Breeze* that Mr. C.H. Ludington was willing to donate his old residence (the former Parsons Tavern) for a school and pay to have it moved to a suitable site. This proposal was met with approval from the townspeople, and it was thought quite fitting that Phoebe Griffin Noyes's former home would once again be used as a school.

Evelyn and her husband disclosed that they had made provisions in their wills to fund an institution of higher learning but that in light of Mr. Ludington's offer, they would immediately give a five-acre lot for the school building.

There were several groups of trustees and committees involved, and the process of transferring title and assets became complicated. As time passed with little progress, tensions rose and relations between the different factions grew strained. Meanwhile, the Salisburys had the building renovated to better serve as a school, but the town board of education was unsure it could legally support a private school and wanted to move forward with plans for a public high school under the jurisdiction of the town rather than a board of trustees. On October 1, 1894, the town agreed to erect a Central School in the First District, under the control of the board of education. Evelyn's reaction savored of wry humor tempered by more than a hint of disappointment. She wrote, "When we see what the town of Lyme is doing in the cause of public education, we think we have 'provoked to good works', if not 'to love.'"

Undaunted, in 1896, the Salisburys presented an alternative plan for the proposed school site. They would purchase the property from the trustees of the Lyme High School Association and donate it to the Ladies' Library Association for a library. They also planned to donate a valuable collection of thousands of books from their own library and provide an endowment for future book purchases.

The Ladies' Library Association, which had been collecting money to build a new, centrally located brick building, called a meeting to discuss this proposal and then postponed it, giving Evelyn the impression that they were less than enthusiastic about the offer. In a scathing open letter published in the *Sound Breeze*, Evelyn excoriated the association for its failure to make a commitment and addressed the members' concerns one by one. Regarding the idea that the proposed library's location was too remote, being removed from "the street," she wrote:

The MacCurdy property between the church and railway crossing where within the thirty years have been placed six houses, all but one of them within eighteen years. People have, therefore found their way out of the "street" to build houses, part of them in new localities. The school building, standing in a central position to the population is one block back of a group of houses and…its somewhat retired position, apart from the constant noise and dust of the main street, and from exposure to fire from without, must be regarded, as itself, in favor of its use for a library. The objection of inaccessibility is thus disposed of.

The notion that a fireproof building was required she dismissed as "impracticable" and added a detailed description of the water arrangement for the building. She then stated that if the association members could somehow see their way to making a swift decision expressing "their unanimous wish and request to obtain…a library, we may be induced to reconsider our present decision." She was not optimistic, though, concluding, "It may, however, be best to postpone the opening of the library during our life-times, or, in view of prospective difficulties and obstructions, it may prove best to give up the project altogether and *forever*."

To Evelyn's credit, she did not let any of these frustrations discourage or embitter her. Rather, when the new Phoebe Griffin Noyes Library was opened, she donated a valuable collection of books and chinaware and, upon her death, left an exceedingly detailed will, donating large sums to benefit the library and local educational causes, including a handsome bequest of $5,000 to the Ladies' Library Association. The MacCurdy-Salisbury Educational Foundation was established to provide funding for educational purposes and to grant scholarships to college-bound Old Lyme students, which it continues to do to this day—a fitting memorial to Evelyn's commitment to the education and betterment of the people of Old Lyme.

3

Florence Griswold

Keeper of the Art Colony

Florence Griswold referred to herself as the "Keeper of the Art Colony." She is often cited as its inspiration and muse. Looking at her early life, there was no way to predict that she would be remembered so many years later as the founder and nurturer of "the birthplace of American Impressionism."

Florence was born on Christmas Day 1850, one of three daughters of Helen Powers Griswold and Captain Robert Harper Griswold, a packet ship captain who was sailing the Atlantic at the time. She was raised in the Late Georgian–style mansion known today as the Florence Griswold House. Designed by architect Samuel Belcher, it was built in 1817 for the Noyes family and purchased by Captain Griswold in 1841.

Women of Miss Florence's day were taught to be "accomplished," which meant that in addition to learning basic subjects like reading and the kind of everyday arithmetic required to manage a farm, household or estate, young ladies were taught the social graces. These accomplishments might include dancing, needlework, music, French or art. An accomplished gentlewoman was considered "refined" and thought to have superior potential as a wife and mother. Florence and her sisters were well educated by the standards of the day, having learned music, painting, needlework and French at the Perkins School in New London.

In 1855, Captain Griswold retired from the sea. His health began to fail, and he made some bad investments, which put the family deep into debt. Contemporary sources speak of Captain Griswold as a notoriously charming man with a generous nature, but he was apparently not a very able financial manager. By 1877, the family found themselves in very difficult circumstances. They needed a source of income, and there were very few ways for impoverished gentlewomen to make their living in the late nineteenth century. The ladies opened a school and began accepting day students and boarders in 1878. The captain's health continued to decline, and he died four years later. At the school, Florence taught French and basic subjects, Louise music and Adele painting.

The Florence Griswold Museum history blog reproduced an advertisement for the school that ran in the *New York Herald Tribune* on October 16, 1881: "Mrs. R.H. Griswold and daughters, in their pleasant home, Lyme, Conn., offer to pupils and to young ladies out

Florence Griswold, circa 1870. *Lyme Historical Society Archives, Florence Griswold Museum.*

of school, special advantages for music (vocal, harp, piano, guitar) drawing, and painting."

In 1896, Louise died, followed in 1899 by mother Helen and the confinement of Adele in a mental institution a year later. Now all alone, Florence attempted to make a living selling flowers and vegetables from her gardens and began to take in boarders. Fortunately, her luck was about to change.

The artist Henry Ward Ranger came to stay at her home, seeking tranquil landscape scenes to paint. He quickly became enraptured by the light and color of Old Lyme and, charmed by Miss Florence's air of faded gentility, soon returned with fellow artists in tow. The legendary "Lyme Art Colony" began to take shape. Ranger favored the darker hues and tonal qualities of the French Barbizon School, and it was he who first called Old Lyme "An American Barbizon." In 1903, Childe Hassam arrived, and although there would continue to be a few tonalist painters at Miss Florence's, the primary focus of the colony became Impressionism.

The hallway at the Florence Griswold House served as an impromptu gallery. *Photograph circa 1910, Lyme Historical Society Archives, Florence Griswold Museum.*

In 1912, Florence Griswold was noted as a member of the Old Lyme branch of the Connecticut Association Opposed to Women's Suffrage. It is interesting to contemplate what some of the discussions at the "Holy House" may have been during the Wilson family's last summer in Lyme,

The Harpist (1903) by Alphonse Jongers depicts Florence Griswold. *Florence Griswold Museum, gift of the Lyme Art Association.*

with Woodrow opposed, daughter Jessie staunchly for and Ellen tactfully keeping her opinion to herself.

Florence maintained a close relationship with the Wilsons. She was a guest at Jessie's White House wedding in 1913 and felt comfortable enough with Woodrow to send him an occasional limerick, as well as regular correspondence.

The artists' work was sold from a makeshift gallery in the front hallway and at an annual show held at the library—a fitting use for the building erected as a memorial to Phoebe Griffin Noyes, who had taught art to previous generations. Art critics began writing of the charming enclave of Old Lyme and specifically of Miss Florence's boardinghouse for artists, and crowds of art buyers and tourists began coming to Old Lyme by train to visit "bohemia." Eventually, the artists realized they needed a more permanent exhibition space, and the Lyme Art Association opened in 1921.

Miss Florence's generosity was legendary. Arthur Heming's memoir, *Miss Florence and the Artists of Old Lyme*, is filled with tales of her kindness toward struggling artists and wayward cats. She set a simple but bountiful table, even when she had to buy on credit, and charged a very low rent. She would often "forget" to collect anything at all from impoverished artists.

Heming tells us Florence refused to accept the painting *May Night* as payment from Willard Metcalf, saying it was the best thing he had ever done, she was sure it would be "snapped up" when he showed it in New York and then "everything will be lovely." A beautiful, moonlit view of the Griswold House, *May Night* was indeed snapped up the following winter. It was awarded a gold medal and purchased by the Corcoran Gallery, launching Metcalf's career as a successful artist.

A wealthy collector came to her some years later and asked to buy the William Henry Howe paintings on one of her doors. He named a substantial sum, offering to buy the whole door and then the entire house, but Florence turned him down, saying she couldn't part with any of the paintings that had been given to her, though she desperately needed the money. When Howe heard this, he "swore like a trooper" and said he would "have gladly painted her half a dozen more!"

As many of the artists became famous and wealthy, they began to purchase homes of their own in Old Lyme and the surrounding areas. Heming decided it would be a grand gesture to surprise Florence with the renovation she was always talking about and began writing to successful artists who had stayed at the boardinghouse in their leaner years.

While Florence was visiting friends in New York, the benefactors pooled their resources, with one offering to pay for new carpet, another a new roof, a third new upholstery and furnishings, a fourth a new stove, etc. When Florence returned, she was amazed by the transformation and deeply touched by the affection and loyalty the artists had shown her.

Heming lived at Miss Florence's for ten years. He said, "Her charm as a hostess made her the greatest benefactor Lyme ever possessed. It was she

The circa 1817 Florence Griswold House, 2014. *Photograph by M. Pearson.*

who raised the price of farms and village lots, caused the renovating of old houses and the building of many a new one, made the merchants well-to-do, and brought prosperity to the whole region."

The artists wanted to purchase the house but were outbid by Judge McCurdy Marsh, who allowed Florence to live there until her death in 1937. It was later purchased by the Florence Griswold Association and became the home of the Florence Griswold Museum and Lyme Historical Society. The house was recognized as a National Historic Landmark in 1993 and is part of the Connecticut Women's Heritage Trail. Florence Griswold was inducted into the Connecticut Women's Hall of Fame in 2002.

4

Ladies of the Art Colony

ELLEN AXSON WILSON

Ellen Axson Wilson discovered the tranquil landscape of Old Lyme as a guest and resident artist at Miss Florence Griswold's boardinghouse. Born in Savannah in 1860, she studied art with Helen Fairchild at the Rome Female College in Georgia. At age eighteen, Ellen won a bronze medal at the Paris International Exposition for freehand drawing, which made her something of a local celebrity. She began to receive commissions for crayon and pencil portraits and eventually went on to study at the Art Students League in New York.

At the Art Students League on West Fourteenth Street, Ellen was able to study with some of the leading artists of the day, including George de Forest Brush and Julien Alden Weir. She took classes in charcoal portraiture, sketching and advanced painting. At the time, the Art Students League was considered a fairly radical organization, as it was administered by the students themselves and did not discriminate based on gender or race.

While in New York, Ellen took full advantage of the social, educational and artistic opportunities the city offered. She attended gallery openings and symphony concerts, accompanied by a friend or sometimes even alone, which would have been considered quite daring in her Georgia hometown. Ellen also volunteered her time at the Spring Street Mission School, teaching African American children how to read.

Ellen met Woodrow Wilson in Rome, Georgia, in 1883, and they became engaged a few months later. While she attended the Art Students League, he was pursuing graduate studies at Johns Hopkins. As they were both finishing up their studies, the couple began making plans for the future. Although Ellen had been granted admission to the advanced class at the Art Students League, it was difficult for a woman to succeed in the fine art world at that time.

One of her biographers, Kristie Miller, calls Ellen's decision to give up her art career a logical one, saying, "She must have realized that the likelihood of Woodrow achieving his goal was greater than the likelihood of her achieving hers. Ellen's decision to invest her talents and energy in his career was based on her own needs." When Wilson expressed some guilt at Ellen's sacrificing a promising career in art, Ellen "assured him that she retained the option to resume it later in their life together."

The Wilsons were married in June 1885, and Ellen dedicated herself to their home and growing family. Woodrow was named president of Princeton University in 1902, and Ellen put her artistic sensibilities to work restoring the interiors of the President's Mansion to their original 1849

Florentine style. As part of the renovations, Ellen Wilson created a new landscape design for the entire grounds in a more informal style, with a rose garden, rambling paths and cedar trees.

As daughters Margaret, Jessie and Nell grew older, Ellen had more free time and began to paint once more. In 1905, Ellen's younger brother Edward, his wife and son drowned in a tragic boating accident. Ellen

Ellen Axson Wilson. *LC-USZ62-25806, Library of Congress, Prints and Photographs Division.*

was extremely distraught, and Woodrow thought a change of scenery might be in order. On the advice of a Princeton colleague, he arranged for a trip to Old Lyme, where Ellen could immerse herself in her art and enjoy the tranquil surroundings.

The family initially stayed at Boxwood, which was a boardinghouse at the time, while Ellen took painting classes with landscape artist Will Howe Foote at Miss Florence Griswold's house. Ellen returned to Old Lyme with her daughters in 1908, this time staying at Miss Florence's while Woodrow was in Europe. She spent that summer taking a landscape painting class with Frank DuMond and painting en plein-air alongside such noted American Impressionists as Childe Hassam. DuMond even arranged for Ellen to have her own studio, which was a great honor for a student.

Woodrow joined Ellen at Miss Florence's in the summers of 1909 and 1910. He made himself at home sitting with the men at the "hot air table" and described the house as "a perfect artistic curiosity shop, the walls and doors of one room, for example, being painted from end to end with landscapes and figures by men of all stamps, most of them now famous, who have lived there the pleasant, informal life they love, and she [Florence Griswold] permits."

Ellen thoroughly enjoyed her summers in Old Lyme, and most years, she brought the president and/or her daughters along. The girls were considered "good sports" by the resident artists, and Jessie served as a model for one of sculptor Bessie Potter Vonnoh's small bronzes. Woodrow was also well liked by the artists, though they did find him a bit "starchy" and formal, given the breezy ways of the art colony. He could take a joke, though, and there were certainly a few at his expense. Arthur Heming's memoir, *Miss Florence and the Artists of Old Lyme*, reveals that no matter what was on offer for breakfast each morning, Wilson insisted on having shredded wheat. One day, Heming substituted a bowl of "excelsior" packing material for the shredded wheat, which Wilson didn't notice until he attempted a spoonful. When Wilson was governor of New Jersey, he received a formal letter on elegant stationery created especially for the purpose, signed by some of Miss Florence's star boarders, under the heading of "The Lyme Anti-Mosquito Coalition," petitioning him to do something about the "mosquito problem."

In May 1911, Ellen Wilson returned to Old Lyme for the last time. In November that year, Ellen submitted one of her paintings to the MacBeth Gallery in New York, under an assumed name. Her canvas was accepted, and the gallery owner, William MacBeth, became her agent. Another painting, a landscape entitled *Autumn*, was accepted into a juried show at the Art Institute of Chicago and later shown at the Herron Art Institute in Indianapolis. Shortly thereafter, Ellen was granted a one-woman show of fifty landscape paintings at Philadelphia's Arts and Crafts Guild, sold several canvases privately and showed five new works at the Association of Women Painters and Sculptors exhibition in New York. All the income she received from the sale of her work was donated to the Berry School for impoverished children in Georgia.

In 1912, Woodrow Wilson was elected president of the United States, and when the family moved into the White House, Ellen managed to carve out a private studio space of her own, setting up her easel in the renovated rooms on the third floor in the former attic space that Teddy Roosevelt had converted into bedrooms. She was the first professional artist to have a studio in the White House. *Ladies Home Journal* published two of her landscapes.

As First Lady, Ellen continued to paint, even as she kept up a busy round of social obligations, hosting over forty receptions in her first three months at the White House, each with an average guest list of six hundred. She also helped the president with his work, reviewing papers, speeches and reports with him and generally "looking after his well-being."

As the issue of women's suffrage became the focus of significant national attention, Ellen was constantly asked her opinion. She kept herself carefully neutral in public, receiving visits from activists on both sides, though there is strong evidence that she privately supported women's suffrage, due to the influence of her daughter Jessie, a settlement house worker and suffrage advocate.

Amid the many events of the White House social whirl, Ellen also planned and supervised the weddings of two of her daughters during the family's tenure at the White House. On November 25, 1913, Jessie was married to Francis Sayre in the East Room, and on May 7, 1914, Nell married treasury secretary William McAdoo in the Blue Room. The pressures of living in the White House had a serious effect on Ellen's health. She often wrote of the many stresses and anxieties she experienced as First Lady and also expressed concern for Woodrow's health. In March 1914, Ellen suffered a bad fall that left her bruised and shaken. Her health began to seriously decline, and at some point, she was diagnosed with Bright's disease, a terminal illness of the kidneys. She died on August 6, 1914, and was buried in her hometown of Rome, Georgia.

MATILDA BROWNE

Matilda Browne was already an established professional artist when she entered the realm of Miss Florence Griswold's "Holy House" in Old Lyme. Born on May 8, 1869, in Newark, New Jersey, she was considered a child prodigy and studied art with her neighbor Thomas Moran, a noted landscape painter of the Hudson River School. When Matilda was nine, Moran allowed her to visit his studio and eventually encouraged her to try her hand at painting. He recognized her artistic potential, and at age twelve, one of Matilda's paintings was accepted for exhibition at the National Academy of Design in New York.

In 1889, Browne traveled with her mother to France and Holland, where she studied with several distinguished painters, among them Eleanor and Kate Greatorex, Frederick Freer and Charles Melville Dewey. She also studied with Carleton Wiggins in New York, who was known for his paintings of pastoral scenes and animal subjects.

As her talent and professional reputation grew, Matilda became known for her "vigorous brushwork" and panoramic landscapes, which invite the viewer into the scene in a way that seems almost three-dimensional. Her vibrant plein-air painting *Peonies* (circa 1907) depicts a woman in a white dress tending a row of bright pink peonies in Katharine Ludington's garden on Lyme Street. It has been speculated that the mystery woman may indeed be Miss Katharine herself, but alas, no solid evidence has yet surfaced to substantiate this notion.

Browne's animal subjects are painted with a translucent clarity and sense of tranquility. She amassed numerous prizes and awards including the Dodge Prize from the National Academy of Fine Arts in 1899 and awards from the Connecticut Academy of Fine Arts in both 1918 and 1919. Her technique was impeccable, and her fame preceded her, both of which led to her being quickly accepted by the male artists as one of the "circle of friends" at Miss Florence's, a status afforded no other female painter.

Matilda Browne was the only female artist to paint a panel in the house, which was considered a great honor. Her *Bucolic Landscape* is a pair of paintings on the door leading to Miss Florence's bedroom that depicts calves placidly grazing under a tree. Sometime around 1920, she was awarded the ultimate boardinghouse honor: her portrait was added into Henry Rankin Poore's *The Fox Chase* mural painted on the dining room mantel.

The Fox Chase depicts twenty-four of the resident artists in satirical form, running across the fields after a fox. The mural includes many humorous

Matilda Browne, *Peonies* (1907). *Florence Griswold Museum purchase.*

details, with the words "School of Lyme" flanked on either side by a full bottle of mastic varnish and a near-empty bottle of rye whiskey. Browne is shown with her arms raised in the air, apparently shocked by the sight of a shirtless Childe Hassam painting en plein-air. Whether this reflects an actual incident or was simply a caricature, there is no way of knowing. Contemporary accounts suggest that Browne was unlikely to have been unsettled by her fellow artists' shenanigans, though she did occasionally seek refuge from the boardinghouse din by renting a house with her mother and sister at 54 Lyme Street (the Justin Smith House), just a short walk down the street from Miss Florence's. She continued to paint and exhibit in Old Lyme until the mid-1920s.

In 1918, Matilda married Frederick Van Wyck, and the couple lived in New York City and Greenwich, Connecticut. The 1920 and 1930 federal censuses show Matilda and Frederick Van Wyck living at 142 East Eighteenth Street in New York, the same building where Lyme artist Edmund Greacen lived with his family. A glance at the "occupations" entry of the censuses shows many other "artists, writers, actors and publishers" at the same address. In 1932, Van Wyck wrote *Recollections of an Old New Yorker*, which featured Matilda's illustrations. After Frederick's death, Matilda moved to Greenwich, Connecticut, where she died on November 3, 1947, at age seventy-eight.

During her lifetime, Matilda Browne was a highly successful artist, and her work continues to be in demand by collectors today. The newspapers were filled with exhibition notices and praise for her work, such as an article in the *New York Times*, dated Sunday, September 8, 1912, which urged art lovers to make the trip to Old Lyme to see the plein-air paintings in their "proper setting." It begins: "If you would see Lyme pictures aright, go visit them in their birthplace. It is a much more rewarding experience than seeing them in broken ranks in the Winter exhibitions." The article featured a large, three-column photograph of Browne's *Cattle* and said of another of her works, "Matilda Browne's delightful cows in *Sunlight and Shadow* are drawn with singular interest and charm."

Browne's paintings were exhibited at numerous galleries, as well as with the Lyme Art Association, the American Watercolor Society, the Art Institute of Chicago, the Chicago Columbian Exhibition, the Louisiana Purchase Expo, Society of Animal Painters and Sculptors and the National Association of Women Painters and Sculptors, of which she was a founding member.

BESSIE POTTER VONNOH

Bessie Potter "attributed her decision to become a sculptor to a fortuitous visit with her mother to the shop of an Italian plaster caster when she was 14." According to Potter's biographer, Julie Aronson, "The proprietor introduced her to sculptor Lorado Taft, who became her sole acknowledged mentor."

Born in St. Louis, Missouri, Bessie had a very close relationship with her mother, Molly. Her father died in a tragic accident when Bessie was very young, and at the age of two, she was stricken with a crippling illness, requiring painful therapies to strengthen her legs. She recalled, "At the age of ten, the doctor attending gave me up. I heard his death sentence…But instead of dying, I gradually began to get well. Why, no one ever understood."

Potter would be known throughout her life for her commitment, focus and ironic sense of humor, all traits she attributed to her childhood struggles. Perhaps because of all they had been through together, Molly strongly encouraged her daughter's artistic interests and supported her early career however she could. When Taft met Potter in 1886, he was teaching at the Art Institute of Chicago, and she was determined to study with him. Taft saw potential in young Bessie and hired her as his studio assistant to help her afford the tuition. She was only fourteen when she enrolled.

In the late nineteenth century, there were many women students at the Art Institute. Chicago was a boomtown, and there were plentiful openings in the commercial trades for trained artists. Many of these jobs were filled by graduates of the Art Institute, and gender was not considered an issue for skilled workers in the decorative arts.

Bessie was a serious student with a natural feel for sculpture. In June 1890, a group of modeled works she had created was awarded a special prize. She became something of a media darling—the subject of profiles and interviews with newspapers and magazines. In 1891, she traveled to New York, with letters of introduction to the famed sculptors Augustus St. Gaudens, Daniel Chester French and others. Returning to Chicago, she assisted Taft with sculpture pieces for the World's Columbian Exhibition and rented her own studio space in the Athenaeum Building, just down the hall from Taft's. She became known for small, finely detailed statuettes of women called "Potterines." Bessie's sculptures brought her critical acclaim and also commercial success. In 1896, she sculpted *A Young Mother*, now in the collection of the Metropolitan Museum of Art, which says, "It synthesizes impressionistic handling of form with realistic emotion to produce one of the most sensitive studies of the mother-and-child theme in American sculpture."

In 1899, she met Robert Vonnoh at Taft's studio. They began exhibiting in tandem and soon married. The Vonnohs spent summers in Old Lyme and became members of the Lyme Art Association. They often stayed at Florence Griswold's boardinghouse. Bessie wrote to Florence to reserve a room in August 1908, with the following caveat: "Just how long we will stay will depend largely upon the mosquitoes. If they do not drive us away, I would like to stay until September."

The Vonnohs were popular with their fellow artists at Miss Florence's and developed a close friendship with the Wilsons. In 1913, Robert Vonnoh painted a portrait of Ellen Wilson and her daughters, and the Wilsons' daughter Jessie was sculpted by Bessie Potter Vonnoh.

Bessie O. Potter in her studio, 1897. *Library of Congress, Prints and Photographs Division.*

As her fame grew, Bessie began accepting commissions for large public works, mainly fountains, including the Frances Hodgson Burnett Memorial Fountain in Central Park and the Theodore Roosevelt Memorial Bird Fountain in Oyster Bay. Throughout her career, she received many awards, including two bronze medals at the 1900 Paris Exposition. She had a solo exhibition at the Brooklyn Museum in 1913 and, in 1921, became the first woman sculptor to be given membership to the National Academy of Design. Robert Vonnoh died in 1933, and she married Dr. Edward Keyes in 1948. Bessie Potter Vonnoh died in New York City in 1955. She is buried at Duck River Cemetery in Old Lyme.

Lydia Longacre and Breta Longacre

Sisters Lydia and Breta Longacre were born into a prominent artistic family with its roots in Philadelphia. Their grandfather James Barton Longacre was a portrait painter and engraver, best known for his work at the United States Mint in Philadelphia, where he was the chief engraver from 1844 to 1869.

Their father, Andrew Longacre, was an engraver, watercolorist and a Methodist minister. Both men also painted miniatures. Reverend Longacre had a distinguished ministerial career in Philadelphia and Baltimore before returning to New York to assume the pastorship at the Madison Avenue Methodist Church. Their mother was Lydia Eastwick.

Lydia Longacre was born on September 1, 1870, in New York City and Breta in

Lydia Eastwick Longacre.
*J0041920, Smithsonian Commons,
Peter A. Juley & Son Collection.*

Baltimore, Maryland, on August 31, 1887. Lydia and Breta were encouraged to explore their artistic talents from the time they were young girls. Their father taught them to draw, and they had ready access to a plentiful supply of art materials. As their skill grew, they were encouraged to pursue further art studies, and both began painting professionally.

Lydia attended the Art Students League in New York, where she studied with William Merritt Chase and H. Siddons Mowbray. She also journeyed to Paris, where she was instructed by James MacNeil Whistler.

In its notes on Lydia Longacre's painting *The Yard*, the Florence Griswold Museum states that Lydia first visited Miss Florence Griswold's boardinghouse in 1906 and "traveled from New York each summer to paint in Old Lyme. She boarded at the Griswold House until the death of Miss Florence in 1937."

Lydia's work was regularly featured in exhibits sponsored by the American Society of Miniature Painters, at the Lyme Art Association and at many other galleries, including the National Academy and the Art Institute of Chicago. She belonged to a number of prestigious art organizations, including the American Society of Miniature Painters and the National Association of Women Painters and Sculptors.

She won several awards, including the 1939 Medal of Honor from the Pennsylvania Society of Miniature Painters and the 1949 Levantia White Boardman Award for best miniature. One of Lydia's most famous paintings was a beautifully luminous miniature of her sister Breta, done in 1914 and titled *The Blue Kimono*, now in the collection of the Florence Griswold Museum. Lydia died in Old Lyme in 1951.

Lydia's sister Breta also studied at the Art Students League, and her work was likely influenced by her older sister, who introduced Breta to Miss Florence and the Lyme Art Colony. Breta was best known for her New England landscapes and still lifes "in a delicate, impressionistic style." Her painting *Banks of the Lieutenant River* depicts a richly colored autumn scene looking out from the grounds behind Miss Florence's house. She exhibited her paintings in Old Lyme in 1914 and 1915.

Breta married electrical engineer William Alexander Del Mar on January 31, 1918, in New York. They settled in Greenwich and had three children.

She continued to paint and became known as a member of the Hudson School of artists. She participated in exhibitions at the National Academy of Design and was a member of the National Association of Women Painters and Sculptors and the Society of American Women Artists. Breta died at age thirty-five on July 10, 1923.

Breta Longacre, wedding portrait, 1918. *Dr. William E. Chapman collection.*

In 1937, on the fiftieth anniversary of her birth, the Greenwich Public Library held a memorial show of her work. Lydia and Breta Longacre's work was featured in the "Notable Women of Lyme" exhibition at the Florence Griswold Museum in 1985.

5

Emilie M. Sill

Businesswoman and Theosophist

L ife is just one damn thing after another," reads the sign above the entrance to Mrs. Sill's Trumbull Street store in Hartford. Inside, Emilie M. Sill presides over the city's largest stationery store, which also boasts the region's largest collection of theosophical and occult publications for sale.

The year is 1893, and Emilie Sill is one of Hartford's most prominent businesswomen. Running the ever-growing shop by herself, she has recently purchased the first parcel of land in Harry Hilliard's new Socialist beach community in Old Lyme. Soon she will build the first house at Hilliard's Sound View Beach and construct a total of thirteen cottages there, forming the "Sill Colony." By 1912, she will become one of the few women to hold a driver's license and have a car registered in her own name. She is a force to be reckoned with, known for her business and real estate savvy—domains that were heretofore the exclusive province of men.

Born Emilie Friebe in New York City in 1856, Emilie entered a world that was being radically transformed intellectually, economically and socially. Her father, Samuel Friebe, was a tailor, and he and her mother, Catherine, emigrated from Austria after the revolutions of 1848, which inspired Karl Marx's *Communist Manifesto*. Immigrants found refuge and opportunity in New York, with its booming shipping and manufacturing industries. The city was also a hotbed of new ideas. The year before Sill was born, Brooklyn's Walt Whitman published *Leaves of Grass*, which celebrated nature and the common man. That same year, an occultist named Helena Petrovska Blavatsky visited New York. In 1875, Blavatsky and Henry Steel

---

E. M. SILL,

Metaphysical, Theosophical and Occult Literature,

Art Studies,   **General Newsdealer,**

Celluloid Novelties,   *Circulating Library.*

89 TRUMBULL STREET.

Early advertisement for Emilie Sill's bookstore, circa 1894. *From* Trinity College Yearbook.

Olcott founded the Theosophical Society, a precursor to today's "New Age" movement. Emilie would soon come under the sway of these new ideas that flowered at the end of the nineteenth century.

By age fourteen, Emilie worked as a milliner in Hartford where her family had recently moved. At twenty-four, she married Louis B. Sill of Old Lyme. Louis was a bookkeeper, and the couple settled in Hartford. Louis became a salesman, traveling as a wholesaler of notions and blank books. In 1891, Emilie set up a shop at 89 Trumbull Street with fifty dollars' worth of stock, introducing a unique element to the elegant world of downtown Hartford: occultism.

Beginning first as a bookstore, Emilie's shop soon included a lending library. Occultism proved to be a good niche market for her. The late nineteenth century was a melting pot of new cultures and ideas. Breaking the bonds of traditional religion and unshackling the economy from the robber barons of the Gilded Age, fresh ideas began to circulate about spirituality, worker's rights and women's equality. The economy was quickly evolving from agricultural to industrial and from rural to urban. The Civil War uprooted an economy based on slavery, upending an arrangement that the South and the major northern port cities had relied on. This ushered in a new age of capital. Enlightenment ideals, upon which the American and French Revolutions were founded in the late eighteenth century, were now coming to fruition in society as a whole.

There was also a more subtle revolution taking place at the time: a revolution of the spirit. A new idea was taking shape in the realm of religion: Theosophy. A spiritual and philosophical movement that was multidisciplinary in its approach and multicultural in its frame of reference, Theosophy sought to combine scientific principles with universal spiritual principles to form a new understanding of the human soul and its place in the cosmos. It grew in influence around the world and found particular acceptance in New England. The Universalist and Unitarian Churches threw their doors open to Theosophy, and by 1894, there were multiple chapters of the Theosophical Society in Connecticut.

How Mrs. Sill first encountered these ideas remains a mystery. But in a two-year period, she took decisive actions that embodied the new philosophy and committed herself to them in a material way. In 1891, the year Madame Blavatsky died, Sill opened Hartford's first theosophical and occult bookstore. She was the sole proprietress, and in the beginning, occult books were not only her specialty—they were her singular stock in trade.

Sill's first business enterprise was a cramped but cozy nook in the heart of downtown Hartford at 89 Trumbull Street. Her store quickly became the mecca for Theosophists and occultists throughout New England. By 1895, newspapers and travel guides were proclaiming, "In this class of literature her stock is second to none in the country." When regular customers requested other items and services, she was quick to oblige. Her bookstore became a noted lending library, lending books to the public for two cents per day. She added all the Hartford daily newspapers and, when those proved popular, added the New York City papers as well, making her shop a must-stop for cosmopolitans. The city of Hartford was possibly the most cosmopolitan place in the United States at that time. It was the wealthiest city in the nation and influential beyond its size. Home to Harriet Beecher Stowe and Mark Twain, it was also the city of modern thinkers like Wallace Stevens, who helped create a new lyrical language for the twentieth century. Sill served the city's sophisticated clientele and became celebrated in her own right, with regular articles in the *Hartford Courant* lauding her appealing personality and business acumen.

As her business flourished, Emilie added her husband's line of stationery and notions to her stock. This proved so popular that it soon became the focus of her store, and she outgrew her shop at 89 Trumbull and rented additional space at the Allyn House, 209–211 Trumbull Street. Her partnership and marriage with Louis dissolved by 1897, and they divorced in 1901, with Emilie citing abandonment as the cause.

In the meantime, Louis started his own stationery store around the corner but would soon leave that line of work altogether, leaving Emilie to take over that space as well. She moved the 89 Trumbull Street store to a larger space at 1181 Main Street but continued to maintain the Annex at 209–211 Trumbull. After the divorce, their only son, Howard Arthur Sill, joined Emilie in the stationery business, managing the Annex.

Auto parade in front of E.M. Sill's Trumbull Street store. *Connecticut Historical Society.*

Between the years of 1897 and 1908, Sill's stores again doubled in size, and she was one of the most important business owners in downtown Hartford.

Being a famous and successful businesswoman also made Emilie Sill a target for thieves and grifters. In the summer of 1905, two men robbed her store, distracting her by sending her to the back to look for a book called *A Long Look Ahead* and then stealing $156 from the cash register while she was away. For a store that began in 1891 with a total investment of $50, we can see how she prospered to have that amount of cash on hand. Emilie was an amiable, kindhearted person, and it was perhaps these qualities that made her a mark for a man by the name of John Kesselman in 1904. Kesselman arrived in Hartford from New York and went door to door asking for work, pretending to be a deaf-mute. In fact, he was a fluent speaker of Yiddish. He was also conversant in sign language, which helped him carry out his various ruses. Though Sill had no work for him, she took pity and let him act as a door-to-door salesman for her wares. She also found accommodations for him and invited him home for meals. Rather than being grateful, Kesselman became belligerent and violent. He badmouthed Sill to her customers and started fistfights in her store. Finally, Emilie had enough and threw him out. Soon, he was arrested and exposed by the Hartford police as a con man.

Perhaps the biggest setback that Emilie Sill faced was a series of suspicious fires. They each occurred a month apart and destroyed much of the Allyn House Annex in 1912. The first was on January 4 at 11:00 a.m. The fire began in the basement and went unnoticed until the newspapers and books at the back of the store went up in flames and caught the attention of Emilie's son, H. Arthur Sill, and a clerk, Hyman Goldberg. When the fire was extinguished and the firemen were leaving, a second fire started under Sill's backroom at 1:30 p.m., and the firefighters returned. When the damage was assessed, Emilie suffered between $13,000 and $17,000 in losses. While the cause of those fires remained unknown, another event occurred exactly one month later on February 4. While the Annex was being repaired, Sill moved what she could and opened for business in a temporary space at 205 Trumbull Street. At about 4:25 p.m., a clerk saw a flash and then an explosive ball of flame in the backroom. The resulting conflagration caused an additional $6,000 in damages. As there were no lanterns or explosive elements in the store, the cause of that fire also remained a mystery. Although the first set of losses was covered by insurance, damages from the February fire were not since the policies were not renewed.

That motto hanging in the window of her store—"Life is one damned thing after another," attributed to socialist-libertarian philosopher and free-love advocate Elbert Green Hubbard—may have been a tribute to Hubbard, or she may have simply liked it because it certainly seemed that in Emilie's life it really was just one damn thing after another.

A circa 1900 advertisement for Emilie Sill's bookstore shows expanded offerings. *From Trinity College Yearbook.*

Fortunately, Emilie had diversified her investments. Income from her real estate helped her recover and get her store up and running again. She also had somewhere to get away from it all. Along with the homes she'd purchased at High Street and Sargent Street in Hartford, Emilie was creating the "Sill Colony" on the beach at Sound View in Old Lyme.

Old Lyme was a world apart from Hartford, but it was a world much of Hartford escaped to in the summer. As the Native Americans had done thousands of years before, the residents of nineteenth-century Hartford packed everything up at the first sign of a heat wave and traveled down the Connecticut River until they reached the Long Island Sound. There, they made their summer homes and enjoyed cool breezes and refreshing swims in the days before air conditioning. In 1893, Emilie was the first investor in Harry Hilliard's new Socialist beach community at Swan Beach, soon to be renamed Sound View. The idealistic Hilliard sold lots to Socialists at a discount, and it's likely that either Hilliard approached Sill as a kindred soul who might be interested in the first purchase or she approached him likewise. It's also possible that Sill just knew a good investment when she saw it and jumped at the opportunity. In any case, from the first tenet of the Theosophical Society, which proclaimed a "Universal Brotherhood of Man," we see that the ideals of these two iconoclasts were in accord.

The beach proved to be a great success. It quickly became known as one of the region's most beautiful resorts, with the finest natural bathing beach on the Connecticut coast. Emilie became a popular figure—her comings and goings regularly noted in the society pages of the *Hartford Courant* and *New London Day*, and her shorefront rentals were filled year after year. Her "Dew Drop Inn" cottage seemed particularly popular. A 1914 article notes a large party from Middletown "making merry" there, "dancing with a Victrola" and "enjoying themselves to the utmost."

In 1916, at the height of her success in the bookstore business, sixty-year-old Emilie decided to sell her store in Hartford and devote herself exclusively to her Old Lyme interests. Her house at Sound View became her permanent residence and the management of her properties a full-time occupation. Her sisters and extended family lived at the Sill Colony with her, as did many guests. Having been a fixture on the beach since its founding, Emilie was always referred to reverently in the accounts of the day.

However, by 1920, the beach was rapidly changing. The onset of Prohibition turned the quiet, genteel getaway into a rowdy stomping ground for rumrunners, bootleggers and shady characters. Perhaps this change, or the cold winters and heavy burdens of multiple property ownership,

A 1906 postcard of the Charter Oak, published by E.M. Sill. *Jim Lampos collection.*

prompted Emilie to sell her Sound View holdings and to take up winter residence in Los Angeles. But California could not match the allure of Old Lyme, and Emilie returned to Sound View each summer, staying with her sister at the Sill House on the corner of Swan Avenue and Shore Road. On August 10, 1934, Sound View's annual Beach Day celebration was dedicated to Emilie, and she was crowned "Queen of the Beach."

Emilie M. Sill moved back to the East Coast and spent her final days in Connecticut. She died in Essex on November 8, 1938, at age eighty-two. She was buried at Cedar Hill Cemetery in Hartford along with some of Connecticut's most notable figures such as Katharine Hepburn and Wallace Stevens, fitting company for a woman who quietly distinguished herself in so many ways.

6

Katharine Ludington

Artist and Suffragist

A rtist, suffragist, founding member of the League of Women Voters and advocate for world peace, Katharine Ludington was one of Old Lyme's most influential figures who gained national recognition in her fight for the rights of women. Born on October 16, 1869, in New York City to wealthy businessman Charles Henry Ludington and Josephine Noyes Ludington, Katharine grew up in New York City and at the family's estate in Old Lyme. Her maternal grandmother, Phoebe Griffin Noyes, was an artist noted for her portraits, and Katharine would follow in her footsteps by becoming an accomplished portraitist herself. She attended the Art Students League in New York City and studied portrait painting at Miss Porter's School in Farmington, Connecticut, under Robert Brandegee. She exhibited in Old Lyme and New York City and at the 1906 Philadelphia Water Color Exhibition and worked as a professional artist for over twenty years.

Ludington would be remembered primarily as a notable Old Lyme painter had it not been for an event in 1914 that precipitated a change in the course of her life that would eventually catapult her into the national spotlight. That year, her brother, Arthur Ludington, died tragically in London, just days before he was to ship off to the front lines of World War I as a Red Cross volunteer. Arthur was a philanthropist and social reformer and had dedicated his life to the service of humanity. A graduate of Yale University, he served as an assistant to Woodrow Wilson when he was president of Princeton University. When Arthur died, he left an estate that was worth over $2.5 million in today's money to his sisters Katharine, Mary and Helen.

Katharine Ludington, circa 1890. *Lyme Historical Society Archives, Florence Griswold Museum.*

He also left Katharine something much greater: a desire to serve a higher cause. Now that he was gone, Katharine dedicated herself to his memory by putting her art aside and taking up the cause of social justice by enlisting in the suffrage movement.

The women's suffrage movement grew out of the abolition movement in the 1840s. In many cases, the same people fought for the emancipation of slaves and the enfranchisement of women. In 1848, antislavery leader Frederick Douglass spoke at the Seneca Falls Convention on women's rights and supported universal suffrage. Elizabeth Cady Stanton, a leading abolitionist who attended the world's first antislavery conference in London in 1840, also spoke at the Seneca Falls Convention and went on to become one of the earliest and most vigorous activists in the women's movement. The passage of the Fourteenth and Fifteenth amendments after the Civil War, guaranteeing equal

Portrait of Josephine Noyes Ludington, painted by her daughter Katharine Ludington. *Old Lyme Phoebe Griffin Noyes Library Permanent Collection.*

protection under the law and voting rights regardless of race, energized the cause of women's suffrage. The notion that black men would be granted rights denied white women lent a new dimension and force to the women's movement. On October 29, 1869, not two weeks after the day Katharine Ludington was born, the first meeting of Connecticut State Suffragists was held at Roberts Opera House on Main Street in Hartford.

As a young woman, Ludington would have been aware of the women's movement, though the cause languished from the 1870s to the beginning of World War I. Slowly, strides had been made as high-profile activists, such as Susan B. Anthony, took to organizing women in the labor force, and over time, the cause gained support. In 1885, the Grange passed a resolution supporting universal suffrage, and in 1890, the American Federation of Labor supported a woman's right to vote. The women's movement dovetailed with the labor movement, Progressive and Socialist politics, as well as social reform movements such as temperance.

It was not until the entry of the United States into World War I that women's suffrage came to the fore in American politics. During the war, as able-bodied men shipped off to fight in Europe, women filled the jobs in factories and offices that the men vacated. Women also served in various capacities on the battlefields of Europe. Proving themselves to be the equals of men in this regard gave further weight to their argument for political equality. The changes brought about by the war in terms of women's rights were eloquently summed up by war veteran Lieutenant Albert M. Simons from Hartford and reported by the *Courant* on March 12, 1919:

> *I was one of those beings who thought woman was inferior, but I have seen the error of my ways; and I believe that confession is good for the soul. In 1917 I was a rabid "anti" but I have learned the rights of women seeing them do men's work on the fields of France. They died beside men and they deserve all the rights that any men have. The army of mothers, wives and sweethearts that stayed behind and fought the fight at home deserve these rights too. I don't know if women will make politics any better, but from what little experience I've had I know that they can't make them any worse.*

Though she attended suffrage meetings as early as 1912, the first record of Katharine Ludington committing to the women's movement came in August 1916, when she attended a meeting as a registered member of the Equal Suffrage League of New London. The meeting was held at Boxwood Manor in Old Lyme, and its featured speaker was the famous suffragist and socialist Katharine Houghton Hepburn. Katharine H. Hepburn, who later became known as the mother of the famous actress from Fenwick, would come to represent a more militant wing of the women's movement. In 1917, she and Alice Paul of the newly formed National Women's Party conducted the first picketing of the White House, calling on President Woodrow Wilson to change his stance opposing suffrage. Through civil disobedience and hunger strikes, Hepburn and Paul used direct action as a tool in the advancement of women's rights. In 1918, Hepburn resigned as president of the nonpartisan Connecticut Women's Suffrage Association to join the Women's Party. In her place, Katharine Ludington was elected president of the Women's Suffrage Association and would soon find herself in the middle of a political storm.

Unlike the firebrand Hepburn, Katharine Ludington approached the cause with a measure of gentility and practiced the fine art of persuasion. Termed by some a "wealthy socialite," by virtue of her family's connections, Ludington moved comfortably in political circles, meeting with governors and congressmen as less a petitioner than a peer. She established a constructive personal rapport with Republican National Committee (RNC) chairman William H. Hays, whom she enlisted to convince Connecticut Republicans to support the proposed "Federal Amendment" also known as the "Susan B. Anthony Amendment," which would enshrine a woman's right to vote in the Constitution of the United States. While the political parties were divided on the issue, in general, Republicans supported women's suffrage while Democrats opposed it. The political lines would be blurred in many cases, however, depending on the local character of each party and the composition of its state leadership. While the national Republican Party supported universal suffrage, the Republican Party of Connecticut opposed it. In particular, Connecticut governor Marcus Holcomb was a staunch antagonist of women's suffrage and employed every device at his disposal to ensure that the amendment did not reach the floor of the state legislature. It was Holcomb's actions through 1919 and 1920 that would thrust the state of Connecticut, and Katharine Ludington, into the national spotlight.

Undeterred by Governor Holcomb's obstructionism, Ludington appealed to RNC chairman Hays to intervene on behalf of Connecticut's women. Throughout the early period of the struggle, she was convinced that by appealing to reason, she could convince Governor Holcomb to become a supporter of women's suffrage, much as activists had successfully convinced President Woodrow Wilson to change his "anti" position and become a voting rights advocate in 1918. Holcomb was a harder nut to crack, and in 1919, Ludington convinced Hays to articulate the Republican Party's clear support of the amendment and thus bring pressure to bear upon Connecticut's leadership. In a personal letter to Katharine Ludington dated December 27, 1919, William Hays wrote, "It is our earnest hope and well founded judgment that the Federal Suffrage Amendment will be adopted and that the women of the country will have the full right to vote for President in every state in the 1920 elections." Through the agency of Hays, Ludington was also a driving force in the RNC resolution that same month that unanimously called upon every Republican governor to hold special sessions of the legislature and expedite the ratification of the suffrage amendment.

Katharine Ludington and Republican national chairman Will Hays. *Library of Congress, Prints and Photographs Division.*

It wasn't just men of the political establishment who opposed women's suffrage. Perhaps an equally potent force opposing the women's vote was women themselves. On November 6, 1912, in the same year that Katharine Ludington first attended a women's suffrage meeting, the Old Lyme Branch of the Connecticut Association Opposed to Women's Suffrage was organized by Mrs. George Ely, and its first meetings were held in her home. Its counterpart, the Lyme Equal Franchise League, was formed on October 30, 1914, stating that "its object shall be to secure the enfranchisement of women of Connecticut." While the pro-suffrage organization allowed men to join as "associate" members, by 1915, Ely's "anti" organization boasted a larger membership role of both active and associate members, though the "anti" organization ironically did not allow men on its rolls at all either as actives or associates. Each organization disputed the other's membership numbers, but what was clear was that the prominent women of Old Lyme were divided on the issue, and female representatives of the region's oldest families found themselves on opposite sides of the question. When Katharine Ludington formally joined the pro-suffrage league in 1916, the doyenne of Lyme's Art Colony, Miss Florence Griswold, was already an active member of the "anti" league.

Why would women be opposed to their own right to vote? The answer is found by exploring where their interests lay. Throughout American history, freedom movements operated on their own logic and defied attempts to reduce them simply to class, race or sex motivation. There is another key factor that must be considered: philosophical and spiritual orientation. What caused white upper-class northern women to support the rights of southern black men in 1830? Or wealthy landed gentry to support the rights of factory workers in 1890? The answer resides in a strain of thought that is uniquely American and pervades American society from its founding. It winds its way across party, class and geographical lines, as well as all other distinctions. It is the philosophy of liberty and social justice. It is the notion that as long as one person is in chains, no other can be free. It informed the Revolution and the transformations to American culture through abolition, temperance, Transcendentalism, Utopian Socialism, Progressivism, Populism and reform. It is founded in the ideas of the Enlightenment and embodied in the actions of activists through the generations. In the end, the common motivation has been how comfortable are you with the status quo of society? In the late nineteenth and early twentieth centuries, if the opinions of any woman counted, they were only those of upper-class women. Women who were actively engaged as leaders in the political arena at this time were primarily educated women from the upper strata of society. Some of these women were conservative and quite cognizant that they benefitted directly from the established structure of society and the political economy; thus, they were quite happy with the status quo. Simply put, suffrage was for them a threat to the social order from which all their privilege derived. But for women who were possessed with a sense of social justice, suffrage was simply a natural extension of the liberation and equality movements they historically had already been involved in, such as abolition and workers' rights, just as the activism of the feminist movement of the late 1960s grew out of the civil rights and antiwar movements from the earlier part of the decade. Thus, for these progressive women, their answer to the question of "How happy are you with the status quo" was, "Not very." As long as there is injustice, there can be no satisfaction.

The evidence of this rift among women of the upper class is clearly evident in the letters they wrote. Susan Platt Hubbard, the chair of the Old Lyme Association Opposed to Women's Suffrage, put a fine point on it in her letter of January 21, 1919, to the *New London Day*: "The policy of the paper is so soundly conservative that it is difficult for me to understand its position on women's suffrage, the most radical and socialistic movement of the day, one that strikes more surely at the foundation of democracy and a representative government than any other of the so-called new movements." On March 24, she wrote, "Does not the *Day* know that Socialist votes gave women in New York the ballot in 1917, and that the Socialist vote in New York increased 133 per cent in 1918, also that the taxpayers of that state must now dig up $2,500,000 for increased election expenses, the cost of the unessential luxury of letting a few women have their own way?" In one stroke of her pen, Hubbard tried to make the women's movement seem selfish and dangerously radical. The rhetoric of the time has a tone that sounds strangely contemporary. In a March 1919 editorial, the *Hartford Courant* complained that "the suffragists are trying to incite disorder and arouse unrest among us and promote sex and class antagonism." The same article reporting on a debate on the floor of the Connecticut Assembly notes that opponents such as Charlotte Howe "predicted racial decadence if suffrage were passed in America."

Suffragists dismissed such charges as ludicrous and rightfully "jeered and giggled at most of the arguments." But the opponents could not be easily laughed off: charges of Bolshevism and incitement of class hatred were made against the background of the Red Scare and the Palmer Raids of 1919. The senseless carnage of World War I upended any notion that humans are rational and moral creatures and called the very foundations of the economic, social, cultural and religious mores of the day into question. In the arts, the reaction to the war was Dada and Surrealism. In literature, there was the hedonism of the Lost Generation. In music, Souza marches and barbershop quartets gave way to hot jazz. In politics, the Russian Revolution of 1917, rising out of the ashes of an autocratic czarist regime that collapsed under the weight of the war, sent shock waves across the Western world. Socialism, which had heretofore been a social reform movement working within the framework of establishment politics, suddenly became a potent force that was gathering international momentum and threatened to overthrow capitalist regimes. The war had temporarily halted the progress of the socialist movement, which by 1912 had Socialist Party presidential candidate Eugene Debs winning 6 percent of the national vote. Indeed, the ties between suffragists and socialists were strong. When Susan B. Anthony met Eugene Debs in 1900, she was reported to have said: "Give us suffrage, and we'll give you socialism." To which Debs replied, "Give us socialism, and we'll give you suffrage." Theodore Roosevelt considered the reform movement that his administration promoted to be the only sensible response to the socialist challenge, adopting many of the socialists' demands in his own programs and blaming the spread of socialism on "the dull, purblind folly of the very rich" who opposed all social reform measures. By 1919, however, with the example of the Russian Revolution fresh in mind, socialism, which had counted Mark Twain, Jack London, Upton Sinclair, Helen Keller, Pledge of Allegiance author Francis Bellamy and other prominent figures in its ranks, came to be regarded as a dirty word. It was erroneously conflated with communism, and both movements were considered to be unpatriotic and un-American. Eugene Debs was jailed for sedition under the Espionage Act, and anyone professing socialist beliefs was possibly subject to the same treatment by President Wilson's Attorney General A. Mitchell Palmer. To accuse women of being "reds" for their support of suffrage was not an idle insult; it was tantamount to accusing them of sedition.

Katharine Ludington would not be so easily classified and was called out by some of her fellow suffragists for being too moderate and unwilling to sufficiently challenge the powers that be through direct action, relying instead on the powers of persuasion. In a letter to the *Hartford Courant* in 1920 after the battle for the vote was won, Katherine Houghton Hepburn noted that Miss Ludington had been "working with infinite patience, industry and effectiveness. Certainly no one could accuse Miss Ludington of militancy!" But Hepburn also went on to say that "in 1917 I became convinced that the policy of the militant suffragists was the only practical one" and that Ludington's Connecticut Woman Suffrage Association "has always been non-militant; so mild, in fact that, in my opinion, women would not be voting now had their policy been followed by us all."

Ludington herself was tarred with "guilt by association" by the opponents of suffrage. The president of the Connecticut Association Opposed to Woman Suffrage, Grace Markham, stated that "they are opposed to suffrage and its alliance with feminism, socialism and Bolshevism" and lumped Ludington in with Hepburn, saying, "Nor can suffragists of the moderate sort disclaim connection with the National Woman's Party. They confer together and work together." But Kitty Ludington would not be baited or have her patriotism questioned. In response to a critic who insinuated that suffragists don't believe "in the old American principle of government by the will of the people," she said, "It is the patriotic women who do believe in that principle who are struggling for woman suffrage because they know that the 'will of the people' can never be expressed when only one-half of that people have the right to express it."

The Ludington House, 2014. *Photograph by M. Pearson.*

Despite divisions among women and within political parties, by 1919, it was clear that universal suffrage would soon be the law of the land. The extension to women of the fundamental rights of citizenship was inevitable, and the arguments against it seemed increasingly transparent and reactionary. But the passage of the Susan B. Anthony amendment guaranteeing a woman's right to vote would not happen smoothly and without struggle, and the epicenter of that struggle would be Katharine Ludington's own state of Connecticut.

The U.S. Congress approved the Nineteenth Amendment to the Constitution on May 19, 1919, and sent it to the states for ratification. Thirty-six of the forty-eight states had to ratify the amendment in order for it to become law, and if women were to vote in the upcoming presidential election, the ratification process had to be completed by September 1920. The process moved quickly. By March 1920, thirty-five of the thirty-six states necessary for ratification had approved the amendment. Confidence in its swift passage was high, and in late 1919, Katharine Ludington was already looking beyond the certainty of ratification and calling for the establishment of an organization that would educate the newly enfranchised voters. In a *Woman Citizen* article, she wrote, "Now that the passage of the Federal Suffrage Amendment seems assured, it is necessary for all of us to face the future with a clear sense of our responsibilities. Connecticut, for the sake of her own welfare, must prepare her new citizens, and we feel that, owing to its extensive organization throughout the state, the suffrage organization is peculiarly fitted to do this work efficiently and economically." A year before the ratification of suffrage, Ludington was already thinking about establishing the League of Women Voters.

It came down to one state in March 1920. Only one more vote was necessary, and as Connecticut had not yet ratified the amendment, the national spotlight turned to Hartford. Katharine Ludington was pleased that her state had the opportunity to cast the deciding vote, and she appealed to Governor Holcomb's Connecticut pride, urging him to call a special session of the legislature to act on the amendment. Holcomb had already refused to do so on four separate occasions, citing procedural questions and protesting that he could only call special sessions in cases of "emergency." Womens' suffrage, in his view, was not such an emergency.

With the weight of the national Republican Party behind her, Ludington was certain that she could persuade Holcomb to change his position, which was not openly "anti" but patronizingly obstructionist. However, she would underestimate Holcomb's resolve. Holcomb, a Freemason whose home was converted into a Masonic Lodge after his death, was comfortable with the notion of government being an elite "boys club," and though he was a Republican, the pressures from the national party or the glare of the spotlight did not affect him. Connecticut was home to some of the nation's most powerful industries, including the brass foundries of the Naugatuck Valley, firearms makers Winchester and Colt in Hartford and the large textile mills along the Quinebaug and Shetucket Valleys. Connecticut's Republican party received much of its support from these industrialists, and it was in no hurry to anger them by supporting a movement that had been so closely allied with labor and socialism. For them, giving women the vote only meant that there would be more support for labor reform and other such inconveniences and impediments to the free rein of business.

Seventy years of struggle were now coming to a head in Katherine Ludington's home state, and as president of the Connecticut Women's Suffrage League, she sprang into action. With the fate of the amendment hanging in the balance, Ludington called for a "Special Emergency Week" on May 3, 1920, to pressure Holcomb into calling for a special session of the legislature. Forty-six representatives of the national women's movement came to Hartford and received their "marching orders and field instructions" from Katharine. Mass meetings and protests were held there, and in Bridgeport, Waterbury, New Haven and New London. The *Woman Citizen* called it the "most dramatic and popular campaign of the seventy-year fight for the enfranchisement of women in the country." Ludington explained her motivations: "This is not an attempt to interfere in Connecticut's private business and in no sense an attempt to coerce the Governor, but the intention is clearly and definitely to open the eyes of state leaders to the fact that Connecticut is obstructing the nation's business. The Governor and his group stand practically alone in refusing to see what the world sees."

Governor Holcomb would not be moved. As the spring turned to summer, the struggle for women's franchisement grew tenser, and the victory that seemed so assured was now slipping away. By August, days before the deadline for ratification, Katharine put aside her usual politesse and let the force of her anger slip through. She penned a coldly sarcastic letter to the *Hartford Courant*, which had steadfastly opposed suffrage, blasting the editors for their hypocrisy, distortion of the facts and blatantly patronizing attitude that called for women to be grateful for all the efforts that were made on their behalf, even if those efforts fell short of the goal. Exposing the reality of the "merry game" that was being played by state Republicans and its supporters on the *Courant* editorial board, Ludington remarked, "We wonder whether the voting women will be so dazzled by these achievements that they will forget the seventy years struggle of women for full democracy and the fact that twenty million American women are still entirely or partially unenfranchised. And we wonder, if by chance the Democratic Party should come along with the thirty six states, whether the women would not set that one decisive and determining act over against the Republican 'almosts' and 'nearlys.'" She added, "we are saving up our gratitude for some real accomplishments." Countering the *Courant*'s claim that "the people of Connecticut are not in favor of the movement," Ludington asked, "What faintest shadow of proof have you for such an astonishing claim," and after setting the record straight about the widespread support both statewide and nationally for suffrage, she wrapped her indignation in an archly amusing paragraph: "The *Courant* has given evidence at times that it possessed a considerable sense of the ludicrous. Was not this saving sense rather off-duty when your editorial was written? You have steadily opposed suffrage in every form. You have stood back of all the efforts of the Republican Party in Connecticut to prevent ratification: and yet from the columns of your paper comes the complaint that Connecticut women are ungrateful for the efforts of the Republican Party on behalf of the suffrage cause! It would be impossible to improve on the irony of this situation."

In the end, Connecticut would not come through. As Katharine hinted in her letter, it was an unlikely candidate, the conservative and Democratically controlled state of Tennessee, that on August 18, 1920, provided the decisive vote that would make women's suffrage the law of the land. Connecticut cynically ratified a month later, when the battle was over and the force of the vote was symbolically meaningless.

Despite the fact that it didn't come in the way that she had hoped, with glory in her home state, Katharine Ludington was nevertheless well prepared for victory. Wasting no time with celebration or self-congratulation, she immediately turned to establishing an organization, the idea for which she first put forth in 1919: the League of Women Voters. Officially founded on April 14, 1921, Ludington served on the board of the League of Women Voters and became its regional director for New England.

The national platform of the league called for an end to illiteracy, support for child welfare, the establishment of a Department of Labor and a Department of Education, promotion of sex education and independent citizenship for married women. It was a nonpartisan organization, and its primary function was to educate newly enfranchised women on the opportunities and responsibilities of full participatory citizenship. It also

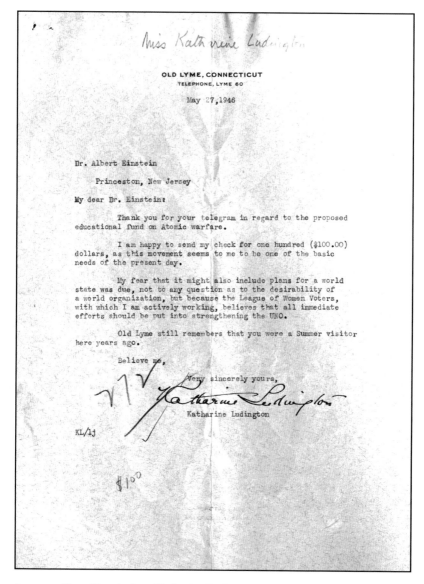

Miss Katharine Ludington

OLD LYME, CONNECTICUT
TELEPHONE, LYME 60

May 27, 1946

Dr. Albert Einstein

   Princeton, New Jersey

My dear Dr. Einstein:

      Thank you for your telegram in regard to the proposed educational fund on Atomic warfare.

      I am happy to send my check for one hundred ($100.00) dollars, as this movement seems to me to be one of the basic needs of the present day.

      My fear that it might also include plans for a world state was due, not to any question as to the desirability of a world organization, but because the League of Women Voters, with which I am actively working, believes that all immediate efforts should be put into strengthening the UNO.

      Old Lyme still remembers that you were a Summer visitor here years ago.

      Believe me,

           Very sincerely yours,

           Katharine Ludington

KL/lj

Letter to Albert Einstein from Katharine Ludington, 1946. *Oregon State University.*

sought to encourage women to enter the political arena, whether for local government boards or higher elected office. Ludington herself was nominated for Connecticut secretary of state by the Democratic Party in September 1920, but with the victory of suffrage behind her, she was destined for work on the national and international stage. Having served its purpose, after fifty-two years in existence, the Connecticut Women's Suffrage League officially disbanded at a meeting held at Ludington's home in Old Lyme on June 10, 1921. As a founder of the League of Women Voters, she now had access and influence at the highest levels of political power, meeting with President Harding in 1921 and attending international conferences on armament limitations.

Katharine Ludington would dedicate the remainder of her life to working for progressive causes, the most central being the League of Women Voters, but also serving on boards of newly formed organizations such as the National Education Association. Founded in 1922, the NEA stood for pacifism and called for increased educational opportunity for all. Its initial focus was the study of the causes of war and the promotion of international peace. At its meeting that year, the NEA declared that "war must be outlawed like the saloon, like slavery." In her note to the Foreign Policy Association in 1923, Ludington wrote that "I am more and more convinced that the average American voter needs to be re-educated almost from the ground up on the prevention of war and the general question of our foreign relation." The cause of international peace remained close to Katharine's heart throughout her life. She was an early and vocal proponent of the League of Nations after World War I and worked to drum up public support for the United Nations after World War II. Little did she know that the failure of Woodrow Wilson's League of Nations was primarily due to the political machinations of her old suffrage ally Will Hays. Along with a small cabal of Republicans, such as Henry Cabot Lodge, Hays worked behind the scenes to sabotage the League of Nations before its basic outlines were even proposed. Indeed, suffrage would be the last noble cause in Hays's resume. In 1921, he was implicated in Harding's Teapot Dome scandal, and taking a side-door exit from politics, he landed a cushy job as the first president of the Motion Picture Association of America at a salary of $100,000 per year. In 1933, he authored the infamous Hays Code, which put a prudish damper on the Hollywood film industry and enshrined the term "Pre-Code" as shorthand for the racy, creative and exciting productions coming out of Hollywood before Hays's wet blanket of censorship.

The League of Women Voters grew in stature and influence throughout the 1920s, and Ludington was instrumental in shaping its policies and direction. Its sponsorship of presidential debates, which the LWV is primarily known for today, arose out of its primary mission to educate the public in a nonpartisan fashion. Ludington's work throughout this period had a lasting influence. In 1928, the league worked with the National

Broadcasting Company to establish a policy of even-handed and thorough political coverage that would serve as the prototype for the subsequent "Fairness Doctrine" and "Equal Time Act." In Ludington's words, the goal of this joint venture between the LWV and NBC would be "to present all sides, to promote none." The need for such a policy was made explicit by Ludington's prescient essay, "Democracy Goes on the Air," published in a journal called *The Survey* on June 15, 1928. In the essay, Katharine predicts the pitfalls of modernity years before the advent of television, the ubiquity of the automobile, the fact of the nuclear bomb or the domination of computers when she writes,

> *Each new invention must be caught and harnessed; there is always the chance that it will run amok. While we were struggling to catch up with steam, electricity was put upon us; then the telegraph, the telephone, and now the radio, with beyond it a dizzy vista of television and who knows what other appalling annihilations of space and time. How to humanize these mechanisms, how to extract the utmost usefulness from them, how to provide against misuse—this is the task which must not be left to chance.*

The Fairness Doctrine and Equal Time laws stood as two of Ludington's legacies, providing guidelines for inclusive and even-handed political coverage in radio and television through the better part of the twentieth century, until the doctrine came under attack and was repealed by the Reagan administration in 1987, and the *Citizens United* decision of the Supreme Court in 2010 finally undid these ideas of fairness and enshrined the notion that money was the sole genius of American politics.

Katharine Ludington's presence continues to be felt in American political culture today, most directly through people she knew and impressed. Famed scholar of southern culture and women's history Anne Firor Scott cites Katharine as being one of her heroes and a "direct influence," calling her "a remarkable woman" and a "mover and shaker." Scott remembers her as being "a grand dame in appearance" who would "come to Washington and sit by my desk and tell me what I ought to be thinking about, having to do with current affairs."

"The Grand Dame of Old Lyme" is also the first phrase that came to University of North Carolina professor emeritus Townsend Ludington's mind when asked to describe his aunt Katharine. Townsend quickly added that although "she acted like that," the title of "grand dame" would have annoyed her, as "her politics were wonderfully liberal." Director of the American Studies Department

A 1921 street fair on Lyme Street. Katharine Ludington, in black, is entering the carriage. *Lyme Historical Society Archives, Florence Griswold Museum.*

at UNC–Chapel Hill for a number of years, he reminisced about growing up in Old Lyme and visiting "Aunt Kitty" on Sundays after church. Luncheons at Aunt Kitty's frequently featured cocktails, and usual guests might include people like Supreme Court justice Felix Frankfurter, who Townsend remembered as wearing "pince-nez" glasses and having "a high squeaky voice." A young boy as his Aunt Kitty was approaching her final years, he was impressed with the fact that his family "thought of itself as an Old Lyme family" and that "Katharine was most connected to Old Lyme." "Aunt Kitty was holding the place together," he recalled and, in a great sense, was keeping the family legacy alive. "She lived alone in that big house, with three servants," tending to her elaborate gardens and overseeing projects near and dear to her heart, including the Phoebe Griffin Noyes Library just a block or so up Lyme Street from the Ludington House. The library was built by her father Charles on the site of her mother's ancestral home, and dedicated to Katharine's grandmother Phoebe Griffin Lord Noyes. Katharine served on the library board for decades and is listed on its rolls in the 1920s as the first subscriber. She was equally dedicated to the establishment and development of Connecticut College, a women's school in New London, about fifteen miles east of Old Lyme.

Katharine was a natural fixture in the town of Old Lyme, secure in her sense of place and family with close friends and associates, such as medical pioneer Alice Hamilton, who lived nearby. Joe Dunn, librarian at Phoebe Griffin Noyes, was a good friend with shared interests, as was Reverend Dixon Hoag of the Congregational Church next door to the Ludington House. Hoag and Katharine "were of the same mind" and "shared political interests"; Hoag "loved her as much as anybody." Dedicated to good works, as was Katharine, Hoag would preach every Sunday at the Women's Penitentiary. Katharine was dedicated to the Congregational Church as well, with the front pew, or "the Ludington Pew," being hers. While she had given up art as a profession after her brother Arthur's death, Aunt Kitty would do sketches for her great-nephew during church services to keep him amused.

The family legacy was very much in the forefront of Katharine's mind, and in 1928, she published a book called *Lyme—And Our Family*, which surveyed the family history. In the descriptions of her ancestors, we can see elements of Katharine's own character and also get a sense of her wit. Katharine noted that her grandmother Phoebe Griffin Noyes possessed a "breadth of mind—a general largesse of outlook, a natural sense of what enriched life" and that she had "an impatience with pretense or affectation of any kind." By contrast, her cousin Evelyn MacCurdy Salisbury, who was also civic minded, exhibited a slightly different character: "Her attitude in later years was that of a dowager countess toward a small English community—the only difficulty being that Lyme people, also keenly conscious of a substantial ancestry and culture, did not see themselves in the role of humble villagers; so Cousin Evelyn's life was a succession of frustrations, accepted usually with good nature and with not the slightest disturbance of a secure sense of superiority." So perhaps it was these two examples of older relatives, the imperious Evelyn and the down-to-earth Phoebe, that helped Katharine maintain a proportionate sense of self in her later years and to live in some accordance with her politics. Though Townsend Ludington remembers her riding in the back of her luxurious, chauffeured Packard convertible, he also remembers that Aunt Kitty would send him to work in the vegetable garden, as "it would be good for him to get his hands dirty."

The gardens of the Ludington House were known for their beauty and were a landmark in Old Lyme. Within the Ludington House gardens was another famous Old Lyme landmark: the Whitefield Rock. Upon this rock in 1745, the avatar of the Great Awakening, George Whitefield, gave his famous sermon to the people of Old Lyme and opened a rift within what had heretofore been the monolithic political and religious enterprise that was the Congregational Church, creating two factions: the New Lights and the Old Lights. Whitefield's New Lights, with their concept of personal salvation, informed and influenced subsequent political movements, such as the formation of Old Lyme's Sons of Liberty in 1766. Indeed, the New Lights of the Congregational Church became the patriots of the American Revolution. Walking through her gardens, pausing at the Whitefield Rock, Katharine could not have been unaware that she stood at the wellspring of a stream that would wind through American history. It was the stream of liberty, and she herself would become part of that stream as it flowed down to a mighty river. Katharine Ludington died on March 7, 1953, and joined her ancestors at the Duck River Cemetery, a short walk from her home. Her epitaph fittingly reads: "Judge me, O Lord, for I have walked in mine integrity."

7

Dr. Alice Hamilton

Medical Pioneer and Peace Activist

Pioneer in industrial medicine, first female faculty member at Harvard Medical School, birth control advocate, social justice crusader and pacifist—Alice Hamilton was a woman of rare talents who applied her gifts tirelessly to the benefit of humanity. She revolutionized the American workplace and nearly singlehandedly set the course for legislation that would protect workers from the lethal hazards they were subjected to in the late nineteenth and early twentieth centuries. A close associate of Jane Addams, she lived at Hull House in Chicago for over twenty years, and there directly experienced the challenges faced by the poor. It was also at Hull House that she first saw many of the industrial hazards she would later fight: the "phossy jaw" of those who worked with phosphorous in the match industry; lead poisoning in various industries but particularly the paint trades; carbon monoxide poisoning in steel mills; mercury poisoning among hatters and thermometer and battery makers; the "dead fingers" and astounding tuberculosis rates among stonecutters; and a host of other hazards from silicosis to poisoning from picric acid, nitrous gas and TNT. Until then, these illnesses were seen as part of the natural order of the American economy, perhaps an unfortunate but necessary side effect of the nation's industrial might, and in most cases, they were attributed to the bad habits and alcoholism of the workers themselves. Patiently and persistently, Alice Hamilton studied each of these diseases, and through her combination of impeccable scientific research and powers of personal persuasion, she managed to uncover their true causes and make effective recommendations for their elimination. Through her work—in which she always placed the personal above the political, the particular above the theoretical and the practical above the ideal—she effectively transformed the way Americans thought about the workplace and, in the course of her efforts, saved countless lives.

Alice Hamilton was born on February 27, 1869, in New York City to Montgomery Hamilton and Gertrude Pond Hamilton. New York was her mother's hometown, but the Hamilton family was based in Fort Wayne, Indiana. Six weeks after she was born, Alice was taken to Fort Wayne, where she was raised. The Hamiltons were a wealthy, well-respected family, standing at the head

Alice Hamilton. *Lyme Historical Society Archives, Florence Griswold Museum.*

of Fort Wayne society. She led a cloistered life with her very close-knit family, which included her three sisters, Margaret, Edith and Norah, as well as her brother, Quint. It was clear that there was something extraordinary about the Hamilton family. Alice's sister Edith became a world-famous classical scholar whose books *The Greek Way* and *Mythology* sold millions of copies and introduced generations to Greek and Roman thought. Her sister Margaret became headmistress at Bryn Mawr, and Norah became an accomplished artist. That these girls would go on to accomplish much directly resulted from their upbringing, during which they were impressed with a sense of high purpose and belief in dedicating oneself to the social good. Alice's mother, Gertrude Pond, was raised in Europe and was, as Alice recalls in her autobiography, *Exploring the Dangerous Trades*, "free from the Victorian prudery which was essential to a lady. She faced sex problems with courage and dignity," and "she taught us that personal liberty was the most precious thing in life." "She could blaze out, even in her old age, over tales of police brutality, of the lynching of Negroes, over child labor and cruelty to prisoners. She made us feel that whatever went wrong in our society was a personal concern for her and for us." It was not only Alice's mother but also her grandmother who helped shape the family's social conscience. Her grandmother was an ardent supporter of temperance and, through that movement, became a supporter of women's suffrage at a time when it was highly controversial to do so. She counted Susan B. Anthony among her personal friends, and Anthony often stayed with the Hamiltons when she was traveling though Fort Wayne.

While the roles of women in the late nineteenth century were circumscribed, they were not restricted to the "home and hearth" of the previous century. Education for girls became a priority for wealthy families, and having a well-educated daughter was seen as a sign of social status. For the first time, women entered the professions, including medicine. Still, the choice between family and career was a mutually exclusive one. One could dedicate oneself to marriage and family or to a life of high moral purpose and social service but not to both. One either married or aspired.

The Hamiltons sent Alice to the prestigious Miss Porter's School in Farmington, Connecticut, in 1886. It was at Miss Porter's that Alice met Katharine Ludington, who would become her lifelong friend and eventually lure her to Lyme. Founder Sarah Porter was a strict Congregationalist who ran her school with "a Christian character." Still, it was socially liberal, and the bonds established among the girls at Miss Porter's lasted for life. Alice would make use of these connections throughout her career.

Upon graduating from Miss Porter's, Alice returned to Fort Wayne for a brief time. It was there that she first discovered Socialism, through the agency of her cousin Agnes and the books of Richard Ely. "Agnes came across Richard Ely's books," Alice recalled. "She was fired with enthusiasm for his program of Socialism and won me over to it easily." The 1890s were a period of hopeful idealism, and Alice gave herself over to this idealism body and soul. She wrote of longing for a world of physical passion but found that she had nothing in common with boys her own age. She considered herself a wallflower and preferred the company of older, well-educated men with whom she could freely speak her mind on a broad range of topics.

Miss Sarah Porter, founder of Miss Porter's School. *Ludington-Saltus Records.*

Uncomfortable in the game of love, Alice chose a life of social service. She selected the field of medicine "because as a doctor I could go anywhere I pleased—to far off lands or to city slums—and could be quite sure I could be of use anywhere." She attended the University of Michigan at Ann Arbor and received her MD in 1893. At Ann Arbor, she received not only a medical education but also a social awakening. While interning at the hospital, she came across a case that shook her to the core and made her reexamine the foundation of her moral judgment. In a letter to Agnes, Alice described the case of "an exceedingly pretty girl" who was "much better bred than the other girls in the ward," but she was "infected with a disease that bad women often have and that renders the approaching confinement very dangerous, almost surely fatal. She is so young, so utterly alone, and has probably been so wicked." Alice was tortured by the fact that, try as she might, she couldn't reach her to establish a personal connection: "Cannot get at her at all. I simply don't know how. I would give anything to reach her. It is all my own fault." Alice found that her attitudes resulting from a strict Christian upbringing flew in the face of what was necessary for her to actually accomplish a genuine Christian act of mercy. It was at this moment that she declared a revolution against herself, resolving to overcome her personal limitations by using all the privileges she acquired by virtue of her social class while discarding the prejudices that came with it. She would root them out from the darkest recesses of her being, through her will and self-conscious efforts, and also materially, by placing herself in the center of the most dangerous and challenging slums. In this way, by relating to people genuinely on whatever level she found them, she could, acting as an equal, hope to effectively make a positive difference in their lives.

In the process, Alice set for herself an impossibly high standard of conduct, and she subjected herself to withering self-rebuke when she couldn't meet it. All praise made her "feel unutterably blue" because it only reminded her of her shortcomings. When her cousin Agnes wrote her praising the heroic work she was doing at the Northwestern Hospital in Minneapolis, where she worked after graduating from Ann Arbor, Alice wrote, "And don't talk about my work in that way again, for it makes me feel like a wretched hypocrite."

While it may be tempting from today's perspective to study Alice's attitude and call it low self-esteem, Alice was in fact holding herself to an exacting standard, one that she could see and aspire to and one she knew was critical to attain if she was to truly accomplish something great. She stood in the fire, trying her soul in the crucible of experience and, in the process, transformed herself into a genuinely empathetic and heroic figure. It was through this personal journey of the spirit that she was able to set the foundation for her work and to bring forth a genuineness, openness and sincerity that would be critical to her effectiveness as an advocate for the oppressed and for the social causes for which she cared deeply not as an intellectual or a "do-gooder" but as a concerned human being.

The process was neither smooth nor easy. In 1893, she moved to Boston to accept a position at the New England Hospital for Women and Children. She detested the bureaucracy of the hospital and the incompetence of its directors. In a letter, she wrote, "Sometimes I am really puzzled to know how far it is right to resist and how far I ought to submit." While she found the atmosphere stultifying—"the place makes me feel as if I were tight-laced and must burst my whalebone for a good, long, breath"—her experiences at Boston began a period when she was meeting influential people with new and challenging ideas that would help light the way for her work. At the New England Hospital, she met Rachelle Slobodinskaya, also known as Dr. R.S. Yarros. A nihilist, Russian revolutionary and early birth control advocate, Yarros was an electrifying figure who made an enormous impression on Alice. Over the next few years, Alice traveled widely, studying in Germany, where she encountered new European ideas, and in 1896, she enrolled at Johns Hopkins Medical School. At Johns Hopkins she found her true love—pathology. Rather than becoming a medical doctor, Alice knew then that being a medical researcher was her true calling. William H. Welch and William Osler, both noted professors of pathology, became her mentors. While at Hopkins, she also encountered Bonte Sheldon Amos, who was part of "the young revolutionary circle" in London, and Amos's friend Alys Pearsall Smith, who was the wife of celebrated philosopher Bertrand Russell. Smith lectured on the virtues of temperance, suffrage and free love. While Alice Hamilton was most sympathetic to the ideals of individual liberation, social reform and economic justice, she couldn't bring herself to agree with the free love movement, which to her was merely the "exaltation of physical existence, or sexual passion, of the primal instincts of man." For her, it was a hedonistic movement that had no place in the great social and economic revolution of the day.

Still, even with her focus on "good works," she took time to ponder the mysteries of love. Ignoring her own situation, she speculated on her friend Katharine Ludington's circumstances in Old Lyme. She wrote, "Kitty's letter was very sweet. She spoke of beginning another winter helping her mother, in a very unselfish way. I wonder if there is some reason why she never has married. Did I tell you that Susan Duryee told me when I was there that she had always imagined Kitty cared for a New York man who used to be a great deal with her and now is not any more. Somehow I cannot but think Kitty could not reach the age of twenty six without falling in love, can you? Of all girls she was the most susceptible." As close as Alice was to Kitty Ludington, she still found Kitty's personal life imponderable. Throughout her life, Alice would keep her own personal life similarly cloaked in the cover of dedication to work and family.

The decisive year in Alice Hamilton's life was 1897, when she accepted a job teaching pathology at Women's Medical School of Northwestern University in Chicago. Even more important than her job was the place of residence she chose upon moving to Chicago. Hull House was one of the first "settlement" houses in the nation and the most influential. Founded by Jane Addams in 1889, Hull House was conceived as "a bridge between the classes." Located in one of Chicago's rougher neighborhoods, Hull House invited young idealistic and educated individuals from the upper classes to live among Chicago's poor and working class and to offer of themselves to the poor either as advocates, teachers or counselors. Alice Hamilton wrote that Jane Addams "offered young people of education and culture and gentle ways a place where they could live as neighbors and give as much as they could of what they had. It is true that Hull House gave them both beauty and comfort, but so far as was possible, they welcomed their neighbors in to share." Addams always maintained that the bridge of Hull House "was as much help to the well-to-do as the poor."

Alice Hamilton met Jane Addams when she spoke at Fort Wayne and, from then on, made it her mission to one day live at Hull House. Alice lived there from 1897 to 1919 and dedicated her evenings and Sundays to settlement work. Intellectually, Hull House became the crossroads of the world for Hamilton. It was there that she heard anarchist Emma Goldman and radical labor leader "Big Bill" Haywood speak. It was there that she befriended Russian revolutionary Prince Peter Kropotkin, whom she found to be a "typical revolutionist of the early Russian type, an aristocrat who threw himself into the movement for emancipation of the masses out of passionate love for his fellow man and longing for justice." Birth control pioneer Margaret Sanger also came through Hull House and won Alice's support. Labor leader Sidney Hillman became a personal friend. More significant were the lifelong bonds she formed with her fellow residents. Along with Addams, Alice befriended Julia Lathrop, who became the first head of the U.S. Child Welfare Bureau of the Health Department, and Florence Kelley, the Marxist social reformer who founded the Consumers League and helped establish the NAACP whom Hamilton described as a "vivid, colorful, rather frightening personality whom I later came to adore." These residents of Hull House—Addams, Lathrop, Kelley and Hamilton— became four of the most effective and powerful social reformers of the early twentieth century.

The most important aspect of Hamilton's life at Hull House was her work with the people of the neighborhood. It was here, living among the poor and working class, where she found a natural way to relate, listen and live on a common level with those she was dedicated to helping. This was an education that she could receive nowhere else: the education of the streets of Chicago, where she discovered a cocaine trade based in drugstores, with druggists trying to hook passing schoolboys on coke. Alice saw the havoc it wreaked on the community; but when she testified at trials as a toxicologist, she found that the druggists were always exonerated. "This was the first in a long series of experiences with our legal system, as carried out in our lower courts, which nearly converted me to anarchism," she wrote. Hamilton also relieved workers on picket lines and felt the terror they faced, walking the lines only early in the day to lessen the chance that she would be brutalized by the police, for whom she had developed a well-founded "deep suspicion and fear." It was also on the streets of Chicago that she witnessed the butchery of back alley abortions, the ostracism faced by single mothers and the oppression faced by women who had large families but had no say in the number of children they would raise. Alice soon realized that, regardless of her religious upbringing, support for birth control was essential to the freedom of women.

It was also on the streets of Chicago that she learned of the "dangerous trades"—the jobs that would leave men injured, maimed, chronically ill or dead. She didn't learn of these horrors through the workers themselves but through their wives. The men were too proud and too scared to discuss their illnesses for fear of being disciplined or replaced. As she put it: "The workers accepted the risks with fatalistic submissiveness as part of the price one must pay for being poor." Alice Hamilton learned a very important technique on these Chicago streets. If you want to find out what's going on in a community, talk to the women. Thus, it was the wives who would tell of the sickness and injuries their husbands faced in the course of their work.

The economy of the United States had been radically transformed by the industrial revolution. By the twentieth century, mills and factories were no longer community-based enterprises, owned by one man who employed local labor or, perhaps, even his family. The country's industrial base had exploded. Factories were now owned by conglomerates or very wealthy men who lived elsewhere. And rather than employ neighbors, the factories now took advantage of an immigrant labor force that was pouring into the nation and a black labor force that was being displaced from the collapsed agrarian economy of the South. The ownership became remote, and the worker had become faceless and expendable. Into this equation was added a drive for greater efficiency and productivity, as well as the introduction of new chemicals whose properties were unknown and old toxins whose dangers were forgotten or ignored. Hamilton noted that immigrant labor "did the heavy, hot, dirty and dangerous work of the country. In return for it they met with little but contempt from more fortunate Americans. The wide open door to let in cheap foreign labor resulted in the building up of great fortunes but measured in terms of human welfare it was cruel and ruthless."

One of the dangers Alice first encountered was mercury poisoning, which was common among hatters and thermometer and battery makers. Mercury poisoning was marked by a jerking of the limbs, swelling, tremors and eventual psychosis. Its dangers had been well known since Roman times. In Spain, it was mandated that "eight days of four hours each" was the equivalent of a full month's work for laborers handling mercury. In this way, as in much of Europe, the hazards of the element were mitigated by limiting exposure. In the United States, there were no such limits, guidelines or regulations. Twelve-hour days, seven days a week were common in industries using mercury. Workers who became sick were cast aside and replaced. Similarly, workers using phosphorous in match factories were offered no protections, even though the dangers of phosphorous were known in the time of Pliny the Elder, who called it "the disease of slaves." In England, the disease was unknown, as the industry was heavily regulated. But the United States was at the height of its laissez-faire capitalism phase, and government regulation was not even a thought in politicians' minds. And so, American workers developed "phossy jaw," a literal rotting of the jaw as a result of their exposure, but they were offered no compensation, relief or recourse.

In the lead trades, most workers lasted four years at the most and then went back to "the old country" to die. As many as one-third suffered lead poisoning, and certain jobs, like maintaining chimney flues, had a lead poisoning rate of 62.5 percent. In the stonework trades, Alice found that stonecutters, using the newly introduced air hammer, not only suffered "dead fingers" but also a stunning tuberculosis rate. The new machinery, as opposed to the hand tools used previously, damaged their nerves and created much more stone dust. Hamilton's research revealed that, among granite workers, there were "more deaths from tuberculosis alone in a period of three years than in the general male population of all causes." Wherever she turned, Alice Hamilton discovered industrial hazards that were poorly understood and completely uncontrolled. Picric acid poisoning, carbon monoxide gassing and silicosis were common. In each case, the cause of the disease was attributed to drinking alcohol or to the worker's slovenly lifestyle. Hamilton noted that the "defense used by the employers was alcoholism. There is no form of industrial poisoning, from lead to dinitrobenzol, from mercury to carbon tetrachloride and nitric acid, which I have not heard some man attribute to whiskey."

Alice Hamilton saw that the best way to help these families was to apply her scientific knowledge to prove the source and cause of their illness. Based on this research, she would appeal to the factory owner's sense of honor and decency to alleviate the problem. Rather than launch a political tirade or publish muckraking articles and exposés that would serve only to bar her from the factories and result in no real reforms, Alice instead hoped to get genuine reforms quietly, on a case-by-case basis, through the power of her impeccable research and personal persuasion with her gentle personality. In this fashion, she charmed her way into factory offices and, presenting her evidence in a nonjudgmental manner, offered practical prescriptions for changes in practices and procedures that the owners often accepted because she worked on their sense of pride and honor. Alice compelled owners to use their own moral standards to improve labor conditions and reminded them that such reforms reflected well on the company as a whole and bolstered its overall reputation. At times, she used her social connections, such as appealing to a schoolmate from Miss Porter's whose father owned a factory she was studying. In each case, Alice used warmth and a human touch over rhetoric and ideology. She learned that employers acted less out of greed or malice than "ignorance and indolent acceptance of things as they are." In most cases, Alice wrote, "the employers could, if they wished, shut their eyes to the dangers." It was her task to open their eyes and to make them see.

When Alice Hamilton began her work, there were no formal studies of workplace hazards in the United States. She became a pioneer in the field, publishing papers that would set the foundation for a new medical discipline: the study of public health. She gained the attention of concerned government officials who were part of the burgeoning social reform movement. In 1908, she was appointed to the newly formed Illinois Committee on Occupational Diseases and charged with the study of lead, phosphorous and benzene in the workplace. In 1910, the governor of Illinois requested that she conduct a formal survey of industrial diseases for the state. Hamilton directed the Illinois Occupational Disease Survey, which was the first of its kind in the

Alice Hamilton. *Lyme Historical Society Archives, Florence Griswold Museum.*

nation. Her focus was on lead poisoning. She was quickly appointed chief investigator for the Illinois State Commission to Study Industrial Diseases—again, this being the first such position established in the nation. In 1911, she became the first occupational disease investigator for the federal government, studying "the canaries" of the munitions works in New Jersey. These were men who had turned yellow from handling picric acid. That same year, she was appointed special investigator to the U.S. Department of Labor, a position she held until 1937. Nearly singlehandedly, Hamilton established this new field of medicine, building its foundation on a case-by-case basis. Hamilton noted that, in 1910, there was no study of industrial disease in the United States. Speaking of articles on industrial poisons, she said that "the number published in American medical journals up to 1910 could be counted on one's fingers." It was up to her to do the research, prove the causes and recommend the remedies. The field was wide open, and her unique combination of sharp scientific intellect and committed social conscience made her an effective advocate for the workers' cause. Through her work, groundbreaking legislation was passed, culminating in the Occupational Health Safety Act (OSHA) that President Nixon signed into law in 1970, the year Alice Hamilton died.

Along with working to mitigate occupational hazards, Alice Hamilton's other passion in life was the cause of world peace. She was an avowed pacifist, and the Western world's descent into a world war in 1914 proved shocking to her. She and her friend Katharine Ludington were so convinced that war was inconceivable that they both left for Montreal on July 31, 1914, to board a ship that would bring them to Europe, where they were to attend conferences. Only three days later, Alice and Kitty watched in utter disbelief as the ship sailed out of Montreal filled not with paying passengers but with the first troops sent to fight in what would be called the Great War. She mourned the loss of innocence: "The period of passionate and hopeful idealism of the '90's" slowly yielded to "increasing disillusion culminating in the shock of war in 1914; [and] of the war years with the intolerance and bitterness and wave of reaction." Disillusioned and dismayed, but not defeated or broken, Hamilton redoubled her efforts to promote peace as the war years progressed. In 1915, she founded the Women's International League for Peace and Freedom with Jane Addams. Together they protested the war to the U.S. Congress, and later that year, they traveled to Europe to register their protest at the Congress of Women in The Hague. Not content to attend a conference in the relative safety of Holland, Addams and Hamilton brought their peace mission directly into the heart of war-torn Europe, visiting Belgium, Germany, Austria, Hungary, Switzerland, Italy and France, where they witnessed the horrors of war firsthand.

After returning to the United States, Alice was lured by Katharine Ludington to the bucolic town of Old Lyme, Connecticut. It was Kitty's home, and Alice had fallen in love with the town over the years as she attended Kitty's annual parties. Alice noted that she "had been a charter member with Felix Frankfurter since 1912 of Katharine's house parties," which attracted artists and intellectuals from all over the area, including Walter Lippman and the other founders of the *New Republic*, Harold Laski, Lord Eustace Percy, Graham Wallas, Manly Hudson, Charles and Mary Beard and the Henry Goddard Leaches. In 1916, Ludington found a lovely house for Alice just up the road from her own estate in Old Lyme. Alice was charmed by the home overlooking the Hadlyme ferry and purchased it. It became her primary residence, and her sisters eventually moved in with her, re-creating the cozy Fort Wayne homestead of their youth. Jane Addams also moved into the Hadlyme cottage upon her retirement from Hull House, and she remained there until her death in 1935.

Alice Hamilton made history again in 1919, when she became the first female doctor on the faculty of Harvard Medical School. She received her appointment to the School of Public Health because it was a growing and important field and, quite simply, because no man was nearly as qualified to teach it. While Alice was justifiably celebrated as the first woman on the

Harvard faculty, her appointment didn't erase discrimination at Harvard overnight. Upon hiring her, Harvard president Abbott Lawrence Lowell made Alice promise that she would not use the Harvard Club, ask for her quota of tickets to football games, march in the commencement or sit on the platform at ceremonies. In other words, Alice was welcome to offer Harvard the benefits of her expertise, but she was not to be seen outside of the classroom. Women were not admitted to Harvard Medical School as students until 1945.

Alice accepted these restrictions with grace and a bit of barbed humor. As in all other aspects of her life, she was more interested in actually accomplishing something rather than grandstanding and scoring points. She was, for example, a committed Socialist and supporter of Eugene Debs, whom she called "a lovable, warm, vivid personality whom I remember as I do few men." Still, her socialist politics did not stop her from working in conservative Republican administrations, such as those of Presidents Harding and Hoover. Once again, politics for her was subordinate to the opportunity to do good, and she kept her progressive notions under her hat as she researched industrial hazards for the federal government. While her politics were known, they were not held against her as it was clear that there was no one else who was as capable or qualified to address occupational hazards. Hamilton would always put fairness and practicality ahead of politics.

Thus, while it seemed surprising at the time, it made sense that Hamilton opposed the Equal Rights Amendment that was introduced in 1920. Though clearly a strong supporter of suffrage and women's rights, Hamilton wrote a scathing letter to ERA advocate Edith Houghton Hooker, saying, "It is only a great ignorance of the poor as they actually are, only a great ignorance of what is possible and what is impossible under our supposed democracy and actual plutocracy, that could make you argue as you do. The vote? Why we are beginning to find that we got almost nothing with it." It was clear to Alice that the ERA would immediately hurt workers, as it would remove the special protections for women and children in the workplace that were so hard won in the Progressive Era. The ERA would erase these gains in the name of equality, but no new protections would be forthcoming. Surveying the political climate of 1920, it was clear to Alice and many others that there was no chance of Progressive labor reform legislation passing in Congress anytime soon. The ERA would score political points, but it would in reality irrevocably set back the cause of workers, particularly women. Once again, for Alice, it was the practical accomplishment and not the symbolic gesture that mattered.

In 1924, Hamilton was appointed to the League of Nations Health Committee, and through that body, the first global efforts were made to control epidemics of typhus, malaria, cholera and bubonic plague. That same year, she was invited to the USSR to survey that nation's industrial hygiene. While she found much to admire in the Soviets' protection of workers' health and applauded their reforms—"it is fine to see people all alike and plain and shabby, never to see a flapper with a made up face, to see no rich people and few abjectly poor"—she was still deeply troubled by the increasing oppression and authoritarianism she saw as Stalin tightened his grip on power after the death of Lenin and the purging of Trotsky and other moderates. While unpopular with her progressive friends, she was not afraid even in those heady early days of the revolution to condemn oppression wherever she saw it.

Her letters from Nazi Germany in 1933 are even more chilling in their accurate prognostication. Accepting a fellowship to the Carl Schurz Foundation Exchange, she found herself in Germany just at the moment that Hitler seized power. While she loved the German people and culture, she mourned their complicity in the rise of "Hitlerism" and their fanatic worship of military authority that was first instilled in them by Otto von Bismarck. She dismissed the notion that Germany embraced fascism because of its economic hardships, noting that she witnessed hardships far worse in other countries, including the United States, and these nations did not choose to "set the clock back." Witnessing the persecution of the Jews and the Nazi attack on modern culture, Hamilton saw that Hitler successfully played to the lowest instincts in the German people. First Lady Eleanor Roosevelt invited Alice to the White House to brief her husband, President Franklin Roosevelt, on the Nazi horrors against the Jews. But she also pointed out that Hitler could not act alone, and simple cultural authoritarianism could not sustain the Nazi movement. Even as early as 1933, Hamilton saw that Hitler was supported by an unholy alliance of international industrialists and financiers who saw him as a bulwark against communists, reformers, labor unions, modern culture and Jewish influence. Indeed, without the support of these capitalists—including Americans, such as automaker Henry Ford and Connecticut senator Prescott Bush, scion of the family that gave the United States two of its presidents—it is unlikely that a man like Hitler would have sustained his success.

Alice returned to the United States, teaching at Harvard and conducting research for the Roosevelt administration. FDR would be

Eleanor Roosevelt presents Dr. Alice Hamilton (right) with the Chi Omega Sorority Achievement Award on June 25, 1936. *Lyme Historical Society Archives, Florence Griswold Museum.*

the third president under whom Hamilton served. In 1935, Alice was forced to retire from Harvard and become a professor emeritus. She permanently moved to Hadlyme, where she continued to write, support progressive causes and work for world peace. She wrote long letters to her old friend Felix Frankfurter, trying to understand how it was that the radical lawyer she knew—the defender of falsely accused anarchists and socialists, the supporter of Sacco and Vanzetti—had become one of the most conservative justices of the Supreme Court, blocking Progressive legislation at every turn under the banner of what would come to be known as "strict constructionism." Their polite, thoughtful and tender letters illuminate their views without resorting to recrimination and reflect a mutual respect and understanding of each other. Not that Alice could be swayed; she continued to align herself with radical causes right through the 1960s, supporting civil rights and opposing the Vietnam War.

As she came into her nineties, the accolades began to pour in for Alice Hamilton. The world knew that they had a treasure in Hadlyme. Connecticut College named a dorm after Alice and her sister Edith in 1961. Ever humble, Alice wrote: "Edith's name must come first. It is not only that her writings on Greece and Rome will always be of lasting value, while mine on dangerous trades are already out-moded, but she is the elder sister, her name belongs in the first place." Connecticut secretary of state and future governor Ella Grasso honored Hamilton in 1968, saying, "When Dr. Hamilton began her pioneering, only a few states granted compensations for industrial accidents, but not a single state compensated for industrial disease. It was her driving force that

Alice Hamilton at her Hadlyme home. *Lyme Historical Society Archives, Florence Griswold Museum.*

opened doors to the enactment of just workers compensation laws and turned the deadly sweatshops of the early 1900's into hygienically safe places to work." In 1969, the Bulletin of Miss Porter's School ran this tribute: "A woman who walked with Presidents and miners, with heads of state and ministers, with immigrant workers and the indigent ill, Dr. Alice Hamilton, pioneer doctor in industrial medicine commanded the respect of the obscure and mighty."

Alice died at her Hadlyme home on September 22, 1970, at the age of 101. She was subsequently inducted into the National Women's Hall of Fame, and in 1995, she was honored with a U.S. postage stamp.

8

Josephine Noyes Rotch Bigelow

"The Fire Princess"

Death is our marriage," wrote Josephine Noyes Rotch Bigelow to her consort, the libertine poet and publisher Harry Grew Crosby, the day before they both died in a suicide pact. Harry called Josephine the "Fire Princess," and her brief life became emblematic of the social upheavals and giddiness of the 1920s as her tragic death symbolized the crash that came at the decade's end.

Josephine Rotch was born on July 3, 1908, in New Bedford, Massachusetts, to Arthur G. Rotch and Helen Ludington Rotch. The Rotches were Boston Brahmins. Arthur was from one of Massachusetts's founding families and Helen from a venerable Old Lyme family. Josephine was raised among Boston's elite and educated at Bryn Mawr, but she also had a reputation as a wild child who didn't quite fit in with Boston's buttoned-up society. She was a flapper—a party girl and, in the terms of those days, "a bad egg" whose promiscuity and fresh ideas were frowned on.

Josephine's family were relieved when she announced, at the age of twenty-one, that she would marry Harvard hockey star Albert Bigelow. Albert was also from Boston's upper strata and generally admired by his classmates. It seemed the party girl was ready to settle down and live a respectable life.

In July 1928, a year ahead of the planned wedding, Josephine went to Venice to shop for her wedding trousseau. While at the Lido outside Venice, she met a man who was like no one she'd met before. Harry Crosby was a poet, an American expatriate living in Paris and the founder of the Black Sun Press, an important new literary imprint. Crosby was at the white-hot center

Josephine Noyes Rotch, circa 1929. *Southern Illinois University, Carbondale.*

of the literary revolution; he counted Ernest Hemingway, F. Scott Fitzgerald, Salvador Dalí, Ezra Pound, William Carlos Williams and E.E. Cummings among his personal friends. His Black Sun imprint published James Joyce, D.H. Lawrence, Marcel Proust, Archibald MacLeish, Kay Boyle, Max Ernst, Crane, Pound and Hemingway. But beyond being a writer and publisher on the cutting edge, Crosby lived his personal life on the edge. He and wife Caresse maintained an open marriage, and his lifestyle gave new dimension to the word "libertine." He threw outrageous and lascivious fêtes at his home on the outskirts of Paris. He drank like a fish and smoked opium. He scandalized the bourgeoisie with surrealist gestures like hiring carriage horses and racing them through the streets. Harvard educated and gentle in manner, he was wild at heart, and this combination of civility and savagery was irresistible to Josephine Rotch.

A nephew of J. Pierpont Morgan, Harry Crosby was also from one of Boston's oldest and wealthiest families, raised to follow his uncle's footsteps into the sober world of banking. Crosby embraced Boston society, values and mores and worked hard to succeed, but his attitude changed drastically when he served in World War I. Harry was at the Second Battle of Verdun and witnessed one of history's most horrific events firsthand. The self-satisfied pieties of Boston's blue bloods and the smug cultural superiority of Europe's burghers and aristocrats turned to ash on that battlefield where 750,000 men lost their lives. There, amid the carnage of that senseless war,

Harry became a different person. He returned to Boston a changed man. He found Boston's insular culture stultifying and laughable, calling the city "Drearyville" and the "City of Dreadful Night." The old world—its morals, religion, literature and culture—had perished on that battlefield in Verdun. For a thinking man like Crosby, there were two choices: go mad or create a new world and redefine the meaning of life. He chose the latter.

Over the next decade, Crosby led a revolutionary life wherein he not only completely redefined sexual mores but, more importantly, created a new religion for himself based on art and literature. Meaning would be created through artistic aspiration, and the visionary poets like Baudelaire and Rimbaud would be his new avatars. He courted Polly Peabody, another disaffected member of Boston's ruling class, and convinced her to leave her husband and marry him. Polly married Harry and changed her first name to Caresse. The Crosbys left for Paris to make a new life together.

In Paris, Harry and Caresse gravitated to other members of the "Lost Generation," such as Ernest Hemingway, and eventually they stood in the center of a circle of the most important writers and artists of the early twentieth century. Harry aspired to be a great poet but never quite succeeded in becoming a first-rate writer. He and Caresse did become first-rate publishers with Black Sun and led a flamboyant lifestyle that embodied the exuberance and experimentation of the age. "Please send $10,000 worth of stock," Harry wrote to his family. "We intend to live a mad and extravagant life." He was completely careless with money, giving it away; spending it lavishly on artistic gestures, surrealist acts and outrageous parties; or simply squandering it as a matter of philosophy. But despite his debauched lifestyle, Harry was not dissipated or dissolute. The Black Sun became very successful, with Caresse editing and Harry courting writers; sourcing hand-woven papers, fine inks and rare typefaces; and supervising the small press runs. The books of Black Sun immediately became groundbreaking literary works and were soon coveted as collectibles. Friends who saw them at work found Harry and Caresse "radiant." Along with the parties and the publishing, Harry also read voraciously and learned to fly airplanes. He was, in short, a man in full.

It was this Harry Crosby whom Josephine Rotch met in Venice in 1928. He proved irresistible. Harry had an understanding with Caresse in which both took numerous lovers outside their marriage, and Josephine became not only one of Harry's conquests but also one of his great loves. He called her his "Fire Princess," and for eight days in Venice, the two carried on a torrid affair. Josephine was a woman after his own heart: educated, open-minded and ready to jump off a cliff into the abyss at a moment's notice. They carried on their affair through 1928 and early 1929, meeting in Boston and New York when they could, until Josephine finally had to break it off in June 1929 when she planned to marry Albert Bigelow.

The marriage of Josephine Noyes Rotch and Albert S. Bigelow took place at noon on the summer solstice, Friday June 21, at the Congregational Church in Old Lyme. The *New London Day* termed it "the social event of the season," timed to coincide with the annual Yale-Harvard regatta taking place in nearby New London. It was "one of the prettiest weddings ever to take place at the Congregational Church," which was decorated with cedar trees and urns of peonies. Immediately after the service, a wedding breakfast was hosted by Josephine's favorite aunt, Katharine Ludington, at her home right next door to the church. Aunt Kitty and Mr. and Mrs. Rotch received four hundred wedding guests that afternoon at the Ludington home.

Now married, it was expected that Josephine would live a staid, respectable life in the tradition of her illustrious New England family. She had dropped out of Bryn Mawr to marry Albert Bigelow, and the two settled in the comfortable confines of Boston's Back Bay. It wasn't long however, before Josephine sought out Harry again. By August 1929, only two months after her wedding, Josephine and Harry had rekindled their affair.

Unlike the free and easy Caresse, Josephine was hot-tempered, jealous and possessive of Harry Crosby. She proved to be a thorn in the side of the normally tolerant Caresse. Harry, for his part, had grown even more eccentric, developing a hybrid Christian-pagan religion of sun worship, based on the alchemical concept of the black sun. He also developed a peculiar attitude toward death. In *Hail Death*, Harry wrote,

> *Die at the right time when your entire life, when your soul and your body, your spirit and your sense are reduced to a pin-point, the ultimate gold point, the point of finality…then is the time, and not until then, and not after then (O horror of anticlimax from which there is no recovery)…in order to be reborn, in order to become what you wish to become, tree or flower, or star or sun, or even dust and nothingness.*

Harry and Josephine's affair grew more serious. He dedicated his book of poems *Transit of Venus* to her and even dedicated a substantial portion of his estate to Josephine in his will. In November 1929, Harry and Caresse were returning from Europe on the *Mauritania*, and Josephine bombarded Harry with radiograms on the ship, trying to fix times and places for them to meet.

They met in Boston and caught a train for Detroit, where they spent five days together at the Hotel Book-Cadillac in a twelve-dollar room, eating caviar, drinking champagne and whiskey, smoking opium and making love. On December 7, they left Detroit, with Harry returning to New York and Josephine saying she would return to Albert. But instead of going back to her husband, the Fire Princess followed her prince back to New York and began stalking him. That night, Harry attended a raucous party at Hart Crane's apartment near the Brooklyn Navy Yard. William Carlos Williams, E.E. Cummings and Walker Evans were there, along with sailors invited up off the street. The party carried on through the early hours of December 8.

On December 9, Josephine went to the Savoy Plaza and caused a scene in the lobby, threatening to kill herself if Harry wouldn't see her. He met her, and she handed him a poem she had written for him featuring the line: "Death is our marriage." Perhaps Harry had worked on her mind during their lost weekend in Detroit, or perhaps she had reached her own conclusions; but by now, Josephine was determined to take Harry from Caresse one way or another. In response, Harry made a final entry in his diary that night: "One is not in love unless one desires to die with one's beloved."

On the morning of December 10, Harry and Caresse woke up together in their room on the twenty-seventh floor of the Savoy Plaza. Harry asked Caresse to jump out the window with him: "Give me your hand, Caresse. Let's meet the sun death together." By the end of 1929, jumping out of high-story windows had become commonplace in New York, with ruined Wall Street brokers and financiers throwing themselves to their doom in the wake of the stock market crash that signaled the beginning of the Great Depression. Caresse, however, laughed Harry off, having heard such fanciful talk from him before and, not taking it seriously, put it down to his overly dramatic romanticism. After all, they had already set a date for their mutual death—October 4, 1944, a day that was still some time in the future. There was no sense in rushing things. Little did Caresse know that if she didn't oblige Harry that day, he would find another who would.

That afternoon, Harry was supposed to meet his uncle "Jack" Pierpont Morgan to exchange Christmas presents, but he never showed up at Morgan's home. Instead, he asked his friend Stanley Mortimer if he could use his studio at the Hotel des Artistes. Mortimer was used to lending his room to Harry for his numerous trysts, and at 1:10 p.m., Josephine, whom Harry had previously introduced as "Miss Rotch," showed up at Mortimer's door. Five minutes later, Harry showed up, drunk, with a fresh bottle of Scotch in tow. By the time Mortimer left them at 4:40 p.m., Harry and Josephine had polished off the quart of whisky.

Harry was due to meet Caresse, her mother and Hart Crane for dinner that evening, after which they all planned to go to the theater. When Harry didn't show up for dinner, Caresse grew distraught. It was very unusual for him to not keep a date, and he never made Caresse worry unnecessarily. While it was common for him to be found in the company of other women, Harry usually let Caresse know of his whereabouts if not the particulars of his activities. As the hour grew later and Caresse grew more concerned, she telephoned Stanley Mortimer to see if he'd seen Harry that day. When he confirmed that he had, she asked him to check up on Harry. Not showing up for dinner and the theater was most unusual behavior for her husband.

When Mortimer arrived at his studio, he found the door barred from the inside and received no response to his repeated knocks. Finally, he asked the building superintendent to knock the door down with a fire axe. When the door was broken down, Stanley Mortimer discovered a strange and terrible scene.

Harry and Josephine were lying peacefully in bed next to each other, fully clothed. Josephine's head rested on Harry's arm, and there was a bullet hole in her left temple. Harry had a bullet hole in his right temple, and in his right hand, he still clutched the gun that fired the shots—a .25-caliber automatic Belgian revolver, with a sun emblem engraved on the handle. They were both barefoot, and Harry's toenails were painted red. He had a Christian cross tattooed on the sole of one foot and a pagan sun symbol on the other. Crushed, on the floor, was Harry's gold "sun ring": a token of his dedication to Caresse that he'd promised he'd never remove.

Mortimer immediately contacted Hart Crane at the theater, who broke the news to Caresse. Unable to bear the scene, Caresse called Archibald MacLeish and pleaded with him to go to the hotel and handle the details. The murder-suicide sent shocked waves through New York, Boston, Paris and the literary community. It was tragic and strange. There was no note and no explanation for the act. It was clearly done in a ritual fashion and meant to convey some occult meaning, but that meaning was not clear.

Exactly what happened in that room on December 10, 1929, and why remains a mystery. It's as much of a mystery as whether Harry and Josephine achieved their final goal of union in immortality. Their friends were not impressed. Though saddened and distraught, they didn't view the act as a statement of love, art or religion—rather as stupid and senseless. The meaning, if there was any, was lost on everyone.

D.H. Lawrence called it "the last sort of cocktail excitement" and of Harry wrote: "He had always been a little too rich and spoilt." E.E. Cummings, Crosby's frequent drinking companion who was with him only two nights prior, callously eulogized the couple in a poem: "2 boston dolls; found with holes in each other's lullaby…the She-in-him with the He-in-her (and both

Grave of Josephine Noyes Rotch, 2014. *Photograph by M. Pearson.*

all hopped up) prettily then which did lie Down, honestly now who go (BANG (BANG." William Carlos Williams was a bit more sympathetic but strangely impersonal when he wrote of them in his poem "The Death of See." Ezra Pound was perhaps the most charitable when he said that Harry and Josephine's end came from "excess vitality" and that their suicide was "a vote of confidence in the Cosmos."

Josephine's husband, Albert Bigelow, saw it quite simply as a brutal murder. Crosby "was a mad poet who lured her to the apartment then murdered her" because she wouldn't submit to him. Edith Wharton, who had always considered Harry "a sort of half-crazy cad," now regarded him as a fully mad cold-blooded killer. Even Kay Boyle, who worshipped Harry while he was alive, viewed him as a mad tyrant after his death. It was clear, though, that Josephine had some degree of complicity in the act. A volume of erotic poems and correspondence between Josephine and Harry was discovered in Katharine Ludington's West Tenth Street townhouse, where Josephine stayed when she was in New York City. Kitty knew nothing about the writing until it was discovered among Josephine's personal effects after her death. In one poem, Harry acknowledged their mutual madness, writing, "My heart is a madhouse for the twin lunatics of her eyes."

Josephine's body was taken back to Old Lyme, and her funeral was held at the Ludington house. Where Aunt Kitty had greeted four hundred of Josephine's wedding guests six months prior, she now hosted those who came to view the coffin and grieve the death of her favorite niece. In the words of the *Milwaukee Sentinel*, "Her bridesmaids of June became her mourners of December." The funeral was presided over by Reverend Hoag, who had also been the minister at the wedding. Josephine was buried in the Ludington family plot in the Duck River Cemetery, near her Noyes, Lord and Ludington ancestors. Her tombstone bears an unusual inscription, one that to this day draws the attention of casual passersby. Though it sounds somewhat biblical, it is not. In fact, it's a play on a few biblical quotations (1 Corinthians 15:54–55; Isaiah 25:8). How and why the inscription was chosen remains unknown, but one cannot help but reflect on Josephine's strange journey when one reads on her gravestone, "In Death is Victory."

9

Elizabeth Tashjian

Artist and Curator

Artist, composer and television personality, Elizabeth Yegsa Tashjian found national fame as the proprietor and muse-in-chief of the Nut Museum in Old Lyme, a unique attraction of her own design.

Born in New York City on December 24, 1912, Tashjian was the daughter of wealthy Armenian immigrants, who divorced when she was seven years old. Her father, Mugurdich, was a prosperous rug dealer, and her mother, Elmas Tikyian, was descended from an aristocratic family.

As a girl, Elizabeth was considered a gifted artist and musician, who played the violin and enjoyed painting. With her mother's encouragement, Tashjian studied painting at the New York School for Applied Design for Women and later graduated from the National Academy of Design, where one of her paintings won a prize.

In 1950, she moved to Old Lyme with her mother, a noted Christian Science "reader," or healer, settling into an elegant Victorian Gothic mansion on Ferry Road. The Tashjians entertained stylishly, and Elizabeth continued to paint, occasionally selling her work at the Lyme Art Association. After her mother's death in 1959, Elizabeth took over the Christian Science healing practice. She had some success but found the work difficult and draining. Elizabeth decided she needed a new project; thus, the Nut Museum was born.

On April 22, 1972, a rainy, blustery day that did not bode well for drawing the hoped-for crowds, the Nut Museum opened to the public and, thanks to Tashjian's bold and frequent press releases, garnered attention

Elizabeth Tashjian. *J0056756, Smithsonian Commons, Peter A. Juley & Son Collection.*

from local and national news outlets, including the *New York Daily News* and *National Geographic.*

A local paper, the *Gazette*, featured the museum several times, including a 1977 page-one story in which Tashjian said she saw the museum as "a means of spreading happiness." She further explained that it is "art, music, history and lore which combine to establish the identity of nuts."

When asked about the museum's purpose, Tashjian quoted from her composition *Nuts are Beautiful*: "Through creative touch/the entity of nuts/is displayed in works of art/to bring joy to all."

Visitors to the Nut Museum entered an exhibition space inspired by Cabinets of Curiosities, an idea that started in the Renaissance but reached the height of its popularity in the nineteenth century. The Victorian-era obsession with collections and curio cabinets that showcased one's interests to friends and visitors was evident in the style and format of the museum.

Elizabeth Tashjian in the front hall of her Victorian home, which housed the Nut Museum. *Photograph by Ellen Land-Weber, 1979; courtesy of Connecticut College Museum Studies Program.*

Tashjian greeted visitors at the door, offered refreshments and collected the admission price of a few dollars plus one nut. She would exclaim over each new nut, asking the donor where they had acquired it and whether it had an interesting history.

Visitors were shown Tashjian's collection of nuts from around the world, plus objects and curios, such as nutcrackers, nut picks, nut bowls and toys made out of nuts. Tashjian's own nut-themed paintings, sculptures and masks were central to the display, from her early still lifes to later work done in an anthropomorphic surrealist style that portrayed nuts and nutcrackers as humanoid forms in swirly dreamlike landscapes. She also created mammoth sculptures of nuts and nutcrackers that were displayed on the grounds of her seventeen-room mansion on Ferry Road.

The elegant structure, with its gabled roof and gingerbread appointments, was the perfect place for such an offbeat attraction, but the heart of the Nut Museum was Tashjian herself, who entertained visitors with stories and songs about nuts, their uses and history. She was particularly proud of her songs, *Nuts are Beautiful* and *Nobody Ever Thinks About Nuts*, which she'd warble a cappella as visitors perused the exhibits.

While considered an eccentric curiosity by some, Tashjian maintained that the Nut Museum was an ongoing piece of performance art, and her persona of the "Nut Lady" was in keeping with this notion, though she much preferred the term "Nut Culturalist." She referred to the museum as a "revelational piece," an ongoing project that she hoped might one day include a gallery building in the shape of a giant walnut and a greenhouse in which to grow nuts.

The Nut Museum was featured on the Connecticut state tourism map and in many guidebooks. *Connecticut Off the Beaten Path* called the Nut Museum "an inspired madness." *Connecticut Curiosities* encouraged readers to visit the museum and quoted Tashjian as follows: "Those who come are prepared for something different…It requires courage to cross the threshold. Once they cross it, they can have a very open mind to get a new look at nuts."

The Nut Museum grew in popularity, largely through Elizabeth's appearances on late-night television. She logged numerous and often lengthy appearances with Johnny Carson, David Letterman, Jay Leno, Howard Stern and Chevy Chase. Tashjian became known to viewers worldwide as the "Nut Lady," a sobriquet which she found both amusing and slightly annoying by turns. She often brought examples of her nuts—most famously a rare Coco-de-Mer, a large thirty-five-pound nut from the Seychelles. The Coco-de-Mer proved a hit with late-night TV audiences, as the diminutive Tashjian slyly called attention to the nut's resemblance to a woman's pelvis and implied that it may have been used in fertility rites. Many visitors to the Nut Museum said they'd come specifically to have a look at Tashjian's famous Coco-de-Mer.

The Nut Museum continued to draw publicity and visitors through the 1990s, but Tashjian increasingly found herself in financial straits. The museum was taken off the Connecticut state tourism map after a motor coach operator wrote that he could no longer bring tourists to the museum because there were squirrels inside the house. Tashjian admitted that there had been a squirrel problem but said she'd had the roof fixed and hoped the state would reconsider. The mansion needed several other repairs and owed thousands of dollars in back taxes. Tashjian's quality of life slowly deteriorated, and visits from social workers and home health aides only served to irritate her. She asked them to leave her in peace.

On May 2, 2002, Elizabeth was found unconscious in her home by a lawyer who had been appointed her conservator. She remained in a coma and spent a month at Middlesex Hospital before being transferred to Gladeview Healthcare in Old Saybrook. Her doctors did not expect her to recover, but she opened her eyes and asked about her home and her paintings, particularly her self-portrait.

Tashjian later said that she had been conscious and aware while she was in the coma and that what had finally awakened her was that she had a vision of someone trying to destroy the self portrait that she had painted many years ago while still living in New York City. In fact, arrangements were at the time being made in preparation for her funeral and the disposition of her effects.

Elizabeth fought valiantly but unsuccessfully to regain ownership of her Old Lyme home, due to a combination of debt and concern for her health and ability to care for herself. As she regained her strength, she continued to create art, referring to her room at Gladeview as "Studio 326." She also used her fame to keep the media interested in her plight, telling the *Hartford Courant*, "How cruel, how merciless to have the state kidnap the Nut Lady."

Many people were concerned about the fate of Tashjian's museum. In 2002, Tashjian's collection of nuts, nutcrackers, nut jewelry and assorted nut-related ephemera were rescued, catalogued and archived, thanks to the efforts of Christopher B. Steiner, a professor of art history and museum studies at Connecticut College. Steiner also saved many pieces of Tashjian's original artwork, including two early self-portraits. The massive nutcracker lawn sculptures were, alas, damaged in a storm but may still be seen in video footage of Tashjian singing her composition "Nuts are Beautiful," which has made her something of a posthumous YouTube star.

Steiner mounted a show of Tashjian's work and artifacts at the Lyman Allyn Museum in New London, which featured a broad swath of Tashjian's artwork, from her early academic paintings at the National Academy of Design to her modern surrealist "outsider" paintings, sculptures and masks from the 1970s to the 1990s. The opening reception drew over 350 people and included an appearance and talk by the "Nut Culturist" herself.

In 2005, director Don Bernier released *In a Nutshell*, a film based on Tashjian's life and work. The film introduces viewers to Elizabeth Tashjian as a person and an artist. It also sheds light on her collapse, startling recovery and fight to recover ownership of her home and artwork.

The film carries the premise that Tashjian was a performance artist and that her artwork, songs and the museum itself were all part of an ongoing piece. Several neighbors and artists appear in the film, with luminous glass artist Mundy Hepburn providing one of the most memorable quotes:

"Elizabeth managed to live like royalty for over fifty years in Old Lyme, on almost no money at all. That in itself is saying something."

Elizabeth Tashjian died on January 29, 2007. She is buried at Duck River Cemetery in Old Lyme. A true original, she was known for fanciful proclamations, such as her oft-repeated philosophy, "Take no thought of the morrow, for the morrow will take thought of the things of itself."

10

Elisabeth Gordon Chandler

Sculptor and Educator

Elisabeth Gordon Chandler was born on June 10, 1913, to Henry and Sara Ellen "Sallee" Gordon in St. Louis, Missouri. Her father worked at Abbott Precious Coin Co., a manufacturer of medals and coins; her mother was a bookseller. When she was young, Elisabeth decided she wanted to "make a difference and bring beauty into the world." She attended private schools in New York and began to focus seriously on her musical career, becoming a professional harpist by eighteen.

Elisabeth began her sculpture career as a hobby by taking classes in artistic anatomy with Robert Beverly Hale at the Art Students League and studying with sculptor Edmondo Quattrocchi, known for his monumental figures in bronze and marble. For a while, she pursued dual music and sculpture careers, touring with the famed Mildred Dilling Harp Ensemble from 1936 to 1946 but also gaining recognition as a sculptor. A December 1946 article in the *Westfield Leader* said of Elisabeth, "She is not only a gifted harpist but has been recognized as one of our best sculptors." From 1940 to 1942, she was Walter Russell's sculpture assistant, working on the *Four Freedoms* monument requested by President Roosevelt.

In the spring of 1945, Elisabeth won first prize in the Brooklyn War Memorial competition for her sculpture *The Victory* in association with architect Stuart Constable, who designed the Memorial Building. At twenty feet high, *The Victory* was designed as the central component of Constable's proposal for the World War II memorial. Elisabeth modeled the face from photographs of Constable's son, an American airman shot down over Germany.

Elisabeth Gordon Chandler with harp. *Elisabeth Gordon Chandler deGerenday Archive, Lyme Academy College of Fine Arts.*

Of *Victory*, Elisabeth said:

> *Following the disaster at Dunkirk and just shortly after Pearl Harbor, I was asked as a student assistant to Walter Russell to design a statue of Victory using a male figure…I conceived* Victory *as a young man rising Phoenix-like from the ashes of war's destruction. The outstretched wing/arms lifting him up are based on the Navajo Eagle Dance, and symbolized American Air Power, without which the war could not be won. The purpose of* The Victory *is not only to immortalize our soldier dead but* [to serve as] *a reminder to the living of the ideals and principles for which they gave their lives. Creating this work was so important to me that I decided to change my profession from concert harpist to sculptor.*

After the competition, Elisabeth went into her studio to complete the working model. When she was finished, six months later, she found that the commission had decided to use the third-place design instead, as it was carved in stone and all bronze casting had been stopped because of the war. Only a small portion of Constable's ambitious design was completed due to a lack of funds. The working model was exhibited at the American Artists Professional League in 1953, the Catherine Lorillard Wolfe Art Club in 1954 and the Lyme Academy of Fine Arts National Sculpture Exhibition in 1996.

Throughout her life, Elisabeth was known for her strong work ethic, persuasiveness and business acumen. She proposed private commissions of prominent individuals and competed for commemorative medals, monuments and portrait busts. In each of her works, she developed a profound connection with her subject through research, interviews and photographs.

She sculpted several medals, including the U.S. Capitol Historical Society's George Washington medal. In 1954, she became the first woman to receive a commission from the U.S. Department of Defense: a portrait bust of James Forrestal, the first secretary of defense. The bust was placed aboard the aircraft carrier USS *Forrestal*. Elisabeth was also asked to create the Forrestal Award Medal, given for "Distinguished Service to National Security."

In 1946, she married businessman Robert Kirkland Chandler, who had a summer home in Hadlyme. In 1962, they moved to Old Lyme, and Elisabeth joined the Lyme Art Association, becoming close friends with many of her neighbors, including aviation pioneer Louise Jenkins and the noted sculptor Alphaeus Cole. Robert Chandler died in 1967.

In 1975, Elisabeth won the commission for an eight-foot statue of Queen Anne, who had granted the royal charter that gave Queen Anne County, Maryland, its name. The eight- to nine-hundred-pound bronze statue took two years to complete and required painstaking research into the queen's life and the fashions and accessories of her day. The scepter, court robes and jewels portrayed are exact replicas of items worn by the queen. Elisabeth portrayed the queen seated in a "Queen Anne" chair with her crown resting on a small period table rather than a regal, crowned standing figure. She holds the charter in her hand and is shown gazing off into the distance, as if imagining the distant colony. At the last minute, Elisabeth added a small spaniel beneath the royal chair, lending an air of homey intimacy. The statue was so large that it had to be cast in several pieces and welded together. It was installed on the Courthouse Green in Centreville and dedicated by Britain's Princess Anne on June 18, 1977.

In May 1979, Elisabeth remarried. Her second husband was the sculptor Laszlo "Laci" de Gerenday. He joined the Lyme Academy faculty, and they taught side by side until his death in 2001.

As a successful sculptor, Elisabeth had her hands filled with commissions for various works, but she had her sights set on something bigger: a School of Art that would teach the fundamentals of painting, drawing, anatomy and sculpture the way they had been taught for centuries. She began speaking with like-minded artists and educators, and in 1976, the Lyme Academy was born as a reaction to the abstract art and "new thinking" that was dominating most schools at the time. Since the rise of modern and abstract art, basic art education in subjects like figure drawing and anatomy had been cast aside in favor of more creative approaches. Figurative art was derided as unimaginative.

But Elisabeth firmly believed that artists needed the skills gained by drawing from the figure and nature as taught from the Renaissance through the mid-twentieth century. She valued figural, representational art and the "old-fashioned" discipline gained through hours in the studio. She thought young artists were being hindered by the lack of formal instruction. They had never had basic training in figure drawing and anatomy and were unable to realize some of their imagined works because they had been taught that the fundamentals didn't matter as much as the innate creativity that inspires a piece. But, Elisabeth asked, what does creativity matter if an artist doesn't have the underlying skills and knowledge to properly execute their design?

In a 1995 interview, Elisabeth said, "I was hoping for the best small school of art. Teaching the fundamentals. Artists need to know the craft before they

Elisabeth Gordon Chandler with her sculpture *The Victory*. *Elisabeth Gordon Chandler deGerenday Archive, Lyme Academy College of Fine Arts.*

can express themselves. So many universities were telling people to sit down and express themselves, without telling them how. It was important to establish a school while there were still a few of us alive who had studied the basics."

The Lyme Academy of Fine Art was started in the basement of the Lyme Art Association (LAA), the gallery built by the artists of the original Lyme Art Colony, on land belonging to Florence Griswold. Chandler had a sky-lit classroom constructed, along with a library, a common room and offices. Two upstairs gallery classrooms were also rented. Elisabeth felt this was a good place to begin, writing in "The Lyme Academy Story," "What more natural place to start a school that returned to the basic fundamentals of art in its teaching?"

In the first year, there were 18 students and 7 instructors, including Robert Brackman of the Art Students League and Tosca Olinsky, a painter and the daughter of Impressionist Ivan Olinsky. Enrollment doubled the following year, but in the third year, the LAA decided not to renew the lease on the upstairs classrooms. So, the school moved to a remodeled garage space nearby. In the autumn of 1981, there were 181 students enrolled.

A series of events then quickly unfolded that led to the school's acquiring its current campus and buildings. The landlord of the garage space raised the rent exponentially, and the LAA basement space became unusable due to a one-hundred-year flood. The school rented classroom space from the town and searched for a more permanent home. The 1817 landmark John Sill House came up for sale and seemed ideally suited to the needs of the growing school, with space for classrooms, a library and a small gallery on a four-acre lot right on Lyme Street, just down the road from the LAA and the Florence Griswold Museum. A capital campaign was undertaken, and funds were raised to purchase the Sill House. By 1984, the school at the Sill House was offering a full curriculum of painting, drawing, sculpture and art history.

In 1994, the Lyme Academy was accredited by the National Association of Schools of Art and Design (NASAD), which allowed credits from the academy to transfer to other collegiate institutions. That September, it offered a three-year undergraduate professional certificate in the fine arts. In the fall of 1995, a full four-year program leading to a bachelor of fine arts degree was offered. In 2001, the academy was recognized as a fine arts college by the New England Association of Schools and Colleges. From then on, the school would be called the Lyme Academy College of Fine Arts.

Elisabeth chaired the Sculpture Department from its founding to her death. She remained deeply involved in her profession into her nineties, teaching a sculpture class once a week and working in her studio. She was available to her students for advice or critiques of their work, and they often praised her method of teaching, in which she would guide them through mistakes or weak points but never actively correct the work itself. This was because she believed that the work should remain entirely the student's, free of the instructor's hand.

Over the years, the college has built additional studios, an academic center and campus housing. In 2014, it became a college of the University of New Haven and is truly thriving. Elisabeth's vision for the school of art she founded has been more than realized, and the original mission remains the same. Her biography on the college's website describes Elisabeth as "a Renaissance woman who firmly but gently led by the example of her own principled life, and who shared with others her boundless generosity and dedication."

Elisabeth Gordon Chandler de Gerenday's work has been exhibited at the National Academy of Design; the National Sculpture Society; the Old State House, Hartford; the Thomas J. Walsh Gallery, Fairfield University; the Paul Mellon Art Center; Lyme Academy College of Fine Arts; the Florence Griswold Museum; and the British Museum, London. She received awards from the National Academy of Design, National Sculpture Society, Allied Artists of America, National Arts Club and Connecticut Governor's Arts Award.

11

The Daring Lady Flyers

Louise Macleod Mitchell Jenkins

Louise Jenkins was an aviation pioneer who flew in competitive air shows and set a record for flying from Montreal to Charlottetown in 1932. Born in Pittsburgh, Pennsylvania, on October 3, 1890, to Samuel Martin "Kier" Mitchell and Margaret Magee Mitchell, Louise Macleod Mitchell was educated at the Shipley School and volunteered to serve as a nurse during World War I.

Her "Emergency Passport Application," filed at the American Embassy in London in 1915, stated Louise's intention to visit the British Isles and France for the purpose of nursing. A renewal in 1917 omitted the return date and simply said she would remain abroad "until the end of the war."

While in England, she met Canadian colonel John S. "Jack" Jenkins, a medical doctor with an interest in flying. They were married in London in December 1918 and returned to live at Jack's family estate on Prince Edward Island (PEI) after the war.

Colonel Jack began flying around 1930 and built an airstrip at Upton Farm. Once it was completed, Louise said, "There seemed to be a constant stream of pilots in and out of the house. Our hallway seemed to be continually filled with the helmets and gear of the pilots using the airstrip. In those days, all planes had open cockpits so you needed helmets and plenty of warm clothes."

Louise Macleod Mitchell in her World War I nurse's uniform, circa 1917. *Uncredited photograph from the* Gazette.

Louise prevailed upon the pilots to take her along and show her how to fly. She said, "You could learn to fly in 5 or 6 weeks if you went every day. I really learned how to fly before I got my license." Her husband had other ideas, however, and insisted she take more formal flying lessons, so she enrolled at a flight school in Montreal and received her license in February 1932.

Louise's plane, a bright red-and-silver DeHavilland "Puss Moth," was considered very dashing. Today, the single-engine Puss Moth may look like a basic craft, but in the 1930s, it was the height of style. One of its innovations was that the pilot's seat was enclosed, not open to the elements. Louise clearly loved her sleek little plane, recalling, "She was always such a happy little ship, and I had nothing but good luck with her."

Louise Jenkins cut quite a dashing figure herself. According to the book *Daring Lady Flyers*, she owned the only Russian wolfhound on the island and also the only Rolls Royce. She was an adventurous soul and avidly embraced the idea of flying. She thought her plane might help publicize her home island and asked that it be given the registration CF-PEI. This request was denied because customized registration numbers weren't allowed, but the determined Louise persisted until the PEI designation was approved by the prime minister himself.

Louise flew her Puss Moth in air shows and pageants and often flew her husband's patients to mainland hospitals, returning with mail and medical supplies. She also used the little plane for long-distance errands, such as dropping her son off for the school term or delivering clean laundry to her daughter at summer camp.

In the early 1950s, Louise moved to Sill Lane in Old Lyme, where she became friends with the sculptor Elisabeth Gordon Chandler, the future founder of the Lyme Academy of Fine Arts. She later moved to Brighton Road, near the Old Lyme Beach Club, of which she was an active member. Her neighbors remember Louise as being a very glamorous and interesting lady.

Amy Roper, who lived on Brighton Road from 1965 to 1972, has fond memories of Louise's bright yellow house, which was "sunny and airy with a detached garage that had a guest loft." "She was a fascinating woman, [who] wore patchouli and made a killer Hungarian goulash. She had classical music playing at all times, [but made an exception] for the Beatles." Roper says she "loved to hear [Louise] talk about piloting planes—she made me realize I could do anything! Louise was the first person I visited when I bought my first motorcycle at age sixteen. She accepted a ride and we took a spin down to the Beach Club and back. She was a very special lady—way ahead of her time."

In 1975, Louise was honored at a ceremonial dinner given by the 99s, an organization of female pilots begun in 1929 that counts Amelia Earhart as a charter member. The name comes from the number of responses that were received after invitations were sent to over one hundred "lady pilots" flying at that time.

At the dinner, Jenkins was given the "Amelia Earhart Award" and recognized for her 1932 record-breaking flight from Montreal to Charlottetown. Her time? Four hours and eight minutes. Of this feat, Louise said, "When I told the dinner audience that I had broken the record and what my time was, they shrieked with amusement. That sophisticated, far-flying group would think nothing of making that same flight now in a third of the time." When she regaled the 99s with stories about flying in the early 1930s, they were "convulsed with merriment" and "looked upon [her] as a sort of flying Methusaleh."

In 1976, Reverend John MacGillivray, a Royal Canadian Air Force chaplain, asked Louise to accompany him as a passenger aboard his vintage 1931 DeHavilland Puss Moth, which he had painted to look just like Jenkins's original, including the CF-PEI markings, in her honor. MacGillivray

Louise Jenkins discusses early aviation with Tom Grasso, Governor Ella Grasso's husband, at Old Lyme's Ella Day in 1975. *Ella Day, Town of Old Lyme.*

had seen Louise Jenkins flying the original PEI in an airshow when he was just fifteen years old and remembered her flying as the inspiration that led him to take up flying himself. MacGillivray later sold the Puss Moth to the Canada Aviation and Space Museum in Ottawa, where it is on display as part of their General Aviation exhibit.

In the early 1980s, Louise told a reporter from the *Gazette*, "Nowadays, everything seems to be so cut and dried, what with all the schedules and such. All you have to do is call an airport and they'll put you on a plane. Flying isn't the same as it used to be."

Louise loved living in Old Lyme and could often be seen at various town events, even in her later years. She was introduced to Governor Ella Grasso at Old Lyme's "Ella Day" celebration in 1975 and shared some stories of early flight with the governor's husband, Tom, who was interested in aviation.

Louise Jenkins died "gracefully and peacefully" at her home at Boxwood Manor on Lyme Street in January 1986. Her obituary requested that memorial donations be given to support the Lyme Academy of Fine Arts, which was founded by her friend Elisabeth Chandler. The obituary also mentioned Louise's friendship with World War II test pilot Cecil "Teddy" Kenyon, who predeceased her by one month.

CECIL "TEDDY" MACGLASHAN KENYON

Cecil "Teddy" MacGlashan was born in New York, the daughter of lawyer Archibald MacGlashan and socialite Cecil Woolsey Hamilton. She was raised in New York and Connecticut and sent to finishing schools in Bermuda and Boston. As a teenager, she was quite a daredevil, much to her mother's chagrin. She pleaded to ride in a barnstormer's plane that had landed in a neighboring field and "borrowed" her brother's motorcycle for a spin whenever she could. While at school in Boston, she met Ted Kenyon, an MIT student who barnstormed on weekends. They were married in 1926, and Ted became a pilot for Colonial Air. Teddy received her pilot's license in 1929 after only ten hours of flight instruction and often served as Ted's copilot. She became an expert flyer, competing in air shows and dazzling the crowds with her bravura performances. She was a charter member of the 99s, the women pilots group.

In 1933, she won the National Sportswomen's Flying Championship at New York's Roosevelt Field, beating twenty-eight men and eleven women for the title. She had borrowed a friend's plane for the competition, and when she won the $5,000 prize, she gave him $1,000 and used the rest of the money to buy a "ship" of her own.

Ted had begun a career as an inventor of aviation and marine instruments, and in 1936, the Kenyons moved to Huntington, Long Island, and formed the Kenyon Instrument Company. Teddy flew many hours as a test pilot for Kenyon Instruments, putting Ted's new autopilot invention through its paces.

Throughout her life, Teddy Kenyon remained committed to the idea that a woman could fly as well as a man. Though she didn't consider herself a "feminist," she was certainly a pioneer for women's rights in the air. Teddy presciently thought the nation's growing number of female pilots could be a valuable asset for the country during wartime and helped organize flying clubs to teach women how to fly.

A 1936 article in the *Lewiston Daily Sun* described these clubs and the role women aviators might play should their service be required: "Mrs. Kenyon… said the women pilots did not expect to do any actual fighting. Rather, they would pilot new planes wherever needed, transport wounded soldiers, carry dispatches and relieve male commercial pilots for fighting service." In 1940, she wrote an article in an aviation newspaper denouncing the Civil Aeronautical Authority's rule that a woman could not fly while pregnant. She pointed out the unfair burden that this rule imposed on women, as it required them to undergo the entire training process again and requalify for their pilot's license after each pregnancy.

Left to right: Teddy Kenyon, Barbara Jayne and Lib Hooker. *San Diego Air and Space Museum Archive.*

With the advent of World War II, Grumman hired Teddy to run an air "ferry service," picking up parts from one place and delivering them to another. She also joined the Civil Air Patrol.

In 1942, Grumman had a shortage of pilots. Bud Gillies, the head of Testing and Flight Operations, offered Teddy Kenyon, Barbara Jayne and Elizabeth Hooker the chance to become production test pilots, flying the company's new warplanes. Grumman closed the airfield on the women's first day, sent most personnel home and invited the press.

The photogenic "lady flyers" were an instant media sensation. Newspapers and magazines featured "glamour shots" of the three in full flight gear—and perfect lipstick. But their day-to-day work was serious business. Not only were the women flying heavy prototype aircraft that required all their skill and training, but they also faced a less-than-welcoming attitude from some of their male co-workers, who felt that "women were not suited for the job." Eventually, the women's dedication, work ethic and skill won over their colleagues.

A retrospective in *New York Newsday* described Kenyon's typical day at Grumman:

> *Each day would begin around 9 am with a long checklist of what had to be tested. With Grumman producing 500 planes a month during the war, there was always plenty of work. The average test run would last an hour. In the air Kenyon would have to go through an intensive drill. On each leg she carried a flight card, documenting engine characteristics: fuel pressure, oil pressure, movement of flaps, precision of hydraulic system and landing gear. She would have to take the plane into a dive at various altitudes to see whether it performed to Navy specifications.*

Teddy tested Grumman's powerful Hellcat fighter plane, which was capable of speeds up to four hundred miles per hour and could reach an altitude of 35,000 feet. A dramatic story is related in the *Newsday* article about a day in 1943 when Teddy was

> *testing a Hellcat at 6000 feet and the left aileron of her plane jammed, greatly hindering its ability to turn. Other test flights were rerouted, while Kenyon tried to get control of the plane. Fire Engines and rescue vehicles were parked on the field…The Tower urged her to fly over the Sound and dump the plane.* [They asked her] *"Do you want to jump?"* but Teddy said *"I wouldn't hurt this aircraft for anything."* Later, Kenyon recalled, *"I couldn't bear the thought of losing that lovely new fighter, so I made a wide turn and lined up with the runway, heading into that nice strong wind."* She landed perfectly.

Teddy was featured in a series of ads for Camel cigarettes during the war years. Wearing her flight gear and standing near a Grumman F6 Hellcat fighter, a glamorously made-up Teddy is shown jauntily holding a cigarette. The ads proclaimed, "I tame Hellcats!" and "That Kenyon Gal can FLY!" "It's Teddy Kenyon—ace woman pilot." The ads proved very popular despite the fact that she "never smoked a day in her life!"

The end of World War II resulted in a lack of orders for warplanes and the return of thousands of men who had worked at Grumman before the war. After two years and thousands of hours logged as a test pilot, Teddy Kenyon was out of a job. She resumed test flying her husband's inventions, and in 1952, the Kenyons moved to Old Lyme. In 1959, she obtained a helicopter license to test Ted's new helicopter gyroscope. She joined the association of women

Teddy Kenyon with Grumman TBM Avenger. *San Diego Air and Space Museum Archive.*

helicopter pilots, the "Whirly Girls." A 1961 article in *Flying* magazine detailed a Whirly Girls event where they were welcomed by Igor Sikorsky to try out the new S-62 helicopter. The *Bridgeport Post* also noted her presence, saying, "Mrs. Kenyon, of Old Lyme, arrived at the Whirly Girls reunion in her own two-seater helicopter, which she landed on the lawn." When the reporter asked her to describe the experience of flying, Teddy said, "Everything diminishes when you're up there. You see your own house looking tinier than a matchbox and you realize that whatever your troubles are, they're just as small. And flying is so beautiful. I love to see the lightning in the sky, the changes of weather, the rain squalls come in and the patterns of the rivers and fields. Everything down below is in proper dimension. Quite small, quite unimpressive."

Teddy continued to fly for the rest of her life, purchasing a small Piper Cherokee in 1970, and in 1977, at the age of seventy-one, she was still flying competitively, as a copilot in the annual New England Air Race, sponsored by the 99s. She died in December 1985.

SHIRLEY WHITNEY TALCOTT

Shirley Whitney was born on October 5, 1918, in Highland Park, California, and grew up in Garden City, Long Island, the daughter of William M. Whitney III and Ruby Yoakum.

In 1943, she wanted to volunteer for service in Europe and had a strong desire to learn how to fly, but her father was deeply concerned for her safety and prevailed upon her not to go abroad. He stayed up the whole night trying to get Shirley to change her mind. Eventually, a compromise was reached, and Shirley decided to join the navy since WAVES weren't then being sent overseas. WAVES, or "Women Accepted for Volunteer Emergency Service," was established in 1942, and its ranks filled a variety of critical positions in aviation, communications and intelligence.

Shirley went to Atlanta for her initial training. She said, "Some people were chosen to work in the control tower, and others on the ground. One of the qualifications was that you had to have very good eyesight to be in the aviation field." After her basic training, she was sent to Chase Field/Beeville Air Station in Texas. She remembers the town of Beeville as so small that it had only one road in each direction, with a single hotel in the middle.

Navy pilots were trained at Beeville from 1942 to 1946. Shirley learned how to fly and remembers flying "all kinds of planes, but mostly dive bombers. Groups of recruits would come in, and we would teach them how to fly. There were probably about 100 women—two barracks full of us! We had what was called the 'Naval Air Link Trainer' [an early flight simulator developed by

Shirley Whitney in her WAVES uniform, 1944. *Talcott family collection.*

Edwin Link]. Each new group would start out on that, before moving up to real planes. The previous trainers were civilians, but they left when the WAVES came in."

Always full of energy and ideas, Shirley started an on-base newspaper to report on daily events. It was a big hit, and the staff obtained permission to stay out past curfew if a few extra hours were needed to produce the next edition. While at Beeville, the women were often called to the main base at Corpus Christi for additional training. Shirley recalled:

> There were three of us who had never flown planes with floats before. This was a special kind of flying done over the water. So we got into the plane and the pilot put us in the Copilot and Navigator seats and goes down his checklist, explaining to us how the plane works. Suddenly he stopped, pointed down at a small light spot in the water and said, "I think we'll have to call him in." Later communication with base confirmed that it was an enemy submarine!

Shirley once had the opportunity to fly a B-24. She explains:

> In April 1944, I was trying to return to my base from leave, and the only flight was filled with officers going to Tennessee, so I hitched a ride with them on a B-24, which is a huge bomber with four engines.
>
> The officers had all been at an event the evening before, and were a little worse for wear. One of the Colonels was the pilot, and they gave me the Copilot's chair, since everyone wanted to sleep. After a while, the pilot also wanted a nap and turned over the controls to me. I flew for a while without incident, then noticed that I wasn't getting the correct signal vector. I quickly woke the pilot, who told me to make a U-turn to go back and search for the signal. I had never flown a plane that large and when I made the turn, we lost about 1000 feet of altitude, which certainly woke up the passengers!
>
> When we reached the base in Tennessee, the Colonel was at the controls, but he asked me to run the radio and contact the tower. The people in the tower were all confused because they didn't have any women pilots at their base, and they couldn't figure out who I was. After we landed, everyone wanted to meet me, and we all went out to dinner together. The next day, I got on another plane that took me back to my base, but that was quite an adventure.

She added, "Traveling around the country on military aircraft was often quite an adventure. In order to take some planes it was necessary to have a parachute with you." Once, after taking trains and aircraft, Shirley found herself in a Cincinnati train station with a crowd of onlookers. The chute she was carrying had deployed and the light silk was trailing behind her across the station hall. "It took a large number of personnel to put it back together, but they did it, right there in the middle of the station."

After the war, most of the volunteer servicewomen went back to civilian life. On a skiing trip with some friends in Connecticut, Shirley met Agnew Allen Talcott. The merry group was invited back to Darien for a party, and the couple stayed in touch, continuing to see each other. They married in 1948 and raised their family in Darien. Shirley became very involved in the Garden Club (their annual President's Award is named after her) and developed a keen interest in environmental causes. She researched the feasibility of establishing a Conservation Commission and helped convince the town of Darien to do so.

The Talcott family had property in Old Lyme, overlooking the Connecticut River, and the couple had always planned to live there full time. Agnew Talcott was the son of Allen Butler Talcott, one of the original Old Lyme Impressionists who boarded at Florence Griswold's house and later purchased an old farm in the area. After her husband's death, Shirley moved to Old Lyme in 1971.

Shirley Talcott devoted much of her life to preserving the environment, working as Chairman of the Nature Conservancy and in the United Nations Office of the Sierra Club. Working with Dr. Richard Goodwin, she helped preserve the Devil's Den Preserve in Weston and Redding and other important tracts of unspoiled habitat in Connecticut.

In June 1972, Shirley was a Sierra Club delegate to the UN Conference on the Human Environment in Stockholm. She also helped the Sierra Club become an accredited nongovernmental organization (NGO). Later that year, she was elected to the executive committee of the new Connecticut Chapter of the Sierra Club.

Shirley was a founding member of the Lower Connecticut Valley League of Women Voters, which, in the 1970s, was very involved in environmental issues, such as the Connecticut River Compact, a study of Long Island Sound, studies on regional land use and planning, transportation and solid waste management in the shoreline towns. In her later years, she moved to Boxwood, where aviation pioneer Louise Jenkins also lived. At age ninety-six, she remains committed to the environmental causes she has supported for so many years. She is an inspirational figure to the younger generation of conservationists and future remarkable women.

12

Ella Grasso

First Elected Woman Governor

Ella Grasso was not just popular with the people, she was truly loved. No politician touched people as deeply as Ella did.
—Hartford Courant, *January 9, 1983*

Ella Grasso, the first female governor in the United States to be elected in her own right, was certainly loved among the people of Connecticut, and nowhere more so than in Old Lyme, where she made her summer home for most of her life. The gauge of her popularity is that over the course of a political career that lasted almost thirty years, she never lost an election. Beginning in 1952, she was elected to two terms in the state General Assembly, followed by three terms as secretary of state beginning in 1958, two terms in the U.S. House of Representatives from 1970 to 1974 and finally a historic victory in the race for governor of Connecticut in 1974, an office she was reelected to in 1978. She didn't just win every race—in most cases the results weren't even close. Though it seems a quaint notion today that any politician could be liked by most of the population, much less "truly loved," for people of a certain age in Connecticut, the simple mention of Ella's name still brings a warm smile.

On May 10, 1919, Ella Giovanna Oliva Tambussi was born in Windsor Locks, Connecticut, to Giacomo (James) and Maria Oliva Tambussi. Ella was the apple of her father's eye. His only child, little Ella grew to be a studious and respectful youngster who also had a bit of tomboy in her. Following her father to work, watching him ply his trade as a baker or accompanying him to baseball games, she was raised with the attention and advantages that were

Ella Grasso, gubernatorial campaign portrait, July 19, 1974. *Library of Congress, Prints and Photographs Division.*

normally accorded only to boys. Her father was a man of Old World traditions, but he believed that a good education was crucial to his daughter's future. Her family pushed her to study and advance herself, but Ella pushed herself even harder to achieve distinction in her academic work. Her mother, Maria, though more emotionally distant, encouraged her daughter's love of reading and was a strict taskmaster, holding her daughter to a high standard that Ella not only met but almost always exceeded.

Growing up as the daughter of immigrants from the Italian Piedmont in the working-class part of Windsor Locks, Ella was not a child of wealth and privilege. Still, through her hard work she won a Rockefeller Scholarship in 1932 to attend the exclusive Chaffee School for girls in Windsor. Though initially uncomfortable among her patrician classmates, Ella excelled in that academic environment and distinguished herself to the degree that an entry in the Chaffee yearbook predicted she would become the first female mayor of Windsor Locks. That particular prediction never came true, but it was only because Ella would become a groundbreaking political figure in a much more dramatic way.

Ella attended Mount Holyoke College on a scholarship and flourished academically. She was inducted into the Phi Beta Kappa honor society, received her bachelor of arts in 1940 and her master of arts in 1942. Ella's time at Mount Holyoke was crucial in her development not only as a student but also as a political citizen. It was at Mount Holyoke that she met Professor Amy Hewes, who would become her mentor. Hewes was a labor reform advocate and pioneer in statistical method who believed in "the equality of people" and "fighting for a better society." Ella found her to be "one of the country's most wonderful women." It was through Hewes that Ella engaged in a formal study of the labor movement and labor conditions in the United States.

Growing up as a child of the Great Depression gave Ella a visceral understanding and concern for the challenges faced by the working class. On a basic level, she appreciated the fact that her father was a baker and not a millworker: "We ate. Some people didn't." On a deeper level, she recalled the shock when the worst effects of the Depression began to be felt on the streets of Windsor Locks and changed the social dynamic of that community. She eloquently summed up her recollections of this time period and how it shaped her view of government:

> *In those days government had a different role in our lives. It was hardly visible and never intruded. And then one day, my mother and I were walking home…it was dark and in our little town of Windsor Locks there was such a chill in the air that it was horrible. The lights in the houses seemed to be dimmed and the banks had closed. This was absolutely traumatic because every penny that anyone had been able to save was there. And then not long after that I watched a family being evicted from their home. I knew the kids. I had gone to school with them and suddenly they were out and everyone looked at them strangely—until other families were evicted too. I watched the WPA and food programs. You know, some of them were not well-managed, but they certainly were well intentioned. They served a very real public purpose and I think it was the first time I realized that the machinery of government can be used for the service of the people.*

The other formative landscape in Ella's youth was the beach community of Sound View in Old Lyme. It was there she met her future husband, Tom, who was a lifeguard. In the summer of 1932, he saw a girl on the beach who caught his attention. She was pretty, but unlike the other girls who were parading and preening, the studious and self-possessed Ella Tambussi was reading Shakespeare's *As You Like It*. The eighteen-year-old Tom was smitten with the fourteen-year-old Ella, and on that day, they began what they would call the world's longest courtship, finally tying the knot ten years later, in 1942, just after Ella received her master's degree from Mount Holyoke. For Ella and Tom, Sound View was a magical retreat in those dark days of the Depression, and at the "Ella Day" celebration Old Lyme threw for the newly elected governor in 1975, Ella recalled that she learned "the basic spirit and purpose of government" from her times at Sound View. As for her approach to politics, she explained it in the terms of a true beach girl: "I don't go around making waves. I just try to find a way through them."

Probably the most decisive political move that Ella made was to join the Connecticut League of Women Voters in 1943. The league was first proposed by Katharine Ludington the year Ella was born, and it was founded a year later. It was designed to help educate women politically and to orient them to the workings of government in order to make the most effective use of the right to vote that they won in 1920. It would give them the tools not only to enjoy the full benefits of citizenship but also to bear the full responsibility of leadership. While Katharine Ludington lived just

Ella Grasso campaign poster atop a vintage voting machine. *Museum of Connecticut History; photograph by J. Lampos.*

down the road from Ella in Old Lyme, the two lived in mutually exclusive circles. The beach communities and the "downtown" part of Old Lyme were worlds apart, literally on the opposite side of the train tracks from each other, and it was rare for "beach" people to socialize with "town" people. "I thought Sound View was the whole boundary of that particular world," Ella recalled. "We never went into Old Lyme." Still, it was the efforts of one of Old Lyme's most prominent citizens, living in that big mansion off the town green at the bend of Main Street (now Lyme Street), that gave Ella not only her start in politics but also the skills she needed to succeed.

The League of Women Voters was "the best political internship possible for an aspiring politician," Ella recalled. It gave her "the most detailed and intimate exposure to the workings of local government," and it inspired her to seek a leadership role. "I think that is why I went into government because I realized early on that if I was concerned with problems, the best way to get them solved was to become part of the decision making process." During her time with the league, Ella served on local boards and commissions and learned the mechanisms of government firsthand. While she would continue to build on this solid foundation of knowledge throughout her career, it was at this stage that Ella first realized that it was critical to learn exactly how government functioned at the realistic, day-to-day, "nitty-gritty" level if she was to make a positive difference in people's lives.

Ella took her first government job at the War Manpower Commission for the State of Connecticut shortly after she married Tom in 1942 and continued in that position until 1946. Her daughter, Susanne, was born shortly afterward in 1948, and her son, James, was born in 1951. While she was a doting mother, having children didn't stop her from pursuing a career in the public sector. In 1948, she began a serious political career working for the Democratic Party. She quickly drew the attention of party boss John Bailey and subsequently became his protégée. In Ella, Bailey saw a unique combination. She was an intelligent Phi Beta Kappa scholar who was comfortable with the state's patrician elite, a working-class girl from the hardscrabble streets of Windsor Locks who understood and related to the troubles and concerns of the average citizen and the daughter of hardworking Italian immigrants who represented all the hopes and aspirations of that community. The Democrats were far outnumbered by Republicans in postwar Connecticut, and Bailey saw Ella as a wedge who could bring excitement and energy into the party. As the "housewife politician," she would represent not only women but also the burgeoning Italian American community that was beginning to flex its political muscle in Connecticut.

In 1952, Grasso was elected to the Connecticut House of Representatives, where she served two terms. She won this first election only a few months before Katharine Ludington died, and in many ways, her victory was the confirmation of the validity of the work that Ludington began all those years ago with the Suffrage League, work which her predecessors had formally initiated at Hartford's Roberts Opera House in 1869. Grasso was thirty-three when she was elected, and she would spend the rest of her life in public service. Her career would culminate in the governorship. Had she lived to see it, Katharine Ludington would certainly have been proud of Ella Grasso's becoming governor, particularly after all the unsuccessful battles Ludington waged for women's right to vote against the retrograde and patronizing Governor Holcomb from 1919 through the frustrating summer of 1920. Not unlike Ludington, once assuming a position of leadership, Ella Grasso sought out a "reasonable" center ground, where support for genuine reforms could be gained through the power of reasonable argument, the art of personal persuasion and the mechanisms of political compromise. In her first election, Ella campaigned as a social liberal and fiscal conservative. She maintained this general orientation throughout her political career.

Ella's time in the General Assembly was marked with notable achievements. From her days in the League of Women Voters, Ella was attracted to the notion of making government more efficient, transparent, representative and responsive. While supporting traditional liberal causes, such as civil rights and assistance for the indigent, elderly and mentally disabled, Grasso also was instrumental in ridding Connecticut of its unnecessary, unwieldy and, in many cases, undemocratic layer of county government. She also championed the new state constitution, which she helped draft and which was ultimately adopted in 1960. While serving as a state representative, Ella kept her eye on a higher prize and received her first taste of gubernatorial politics in 1954 when she worked on Abraham Ribicoff's campaign for reelection.

In 1958, Grasso was elected secretary of state. Ella used the office to reach out directly to the people of Connecticut and made a name for herself as an honest, caring leader. She would be reelected twice, serving until 1970. Voters knew that they could count on Ella to listen to their problems even if she couldn't immediately solve them. She established a toll-free "Ellaphone" that citizens could use to contact her office directly. She kept regular "office hours" at local diners, where she talked to constituents over breakfast—a practice she continued while serving as governor. She also championed "sunshine laws" that would make government documents more available and government decision-making more transparent.

Ella attended the now infamous 1968 Democratic National Convention in Chicago as a delegate and championed a platform to end the war in Vietnam. Outside the convention hall, antiwar protestors had gathered, and in a shocking display of violence and political repression, the Chicago police brutally attacked the demonstrators in a scene that would be televised and witnessed around the world. Respected, mild-mannered newsman Walter Cronkite called the security guards in the convention center "a bunch of thugs." Most famously, in a speech in front of the entire convention that was broadcast live on national television, Connecticut senator Abraham Ribicoff called out the police for their "Gestapo tactics on the streets of Chicago." When the camera cut to the contorted face of an enraged Mayor Richard Daley, the divide in the heart and soul of the United States was plain to see. In June 1968, just a few short weeks before the convention, the frontrunner for the Democratic nomination, Senator Robert F. Kennedy, was shot dead after winning the California primary. His last words were "on to Chicago." America was involved in a controversial war abroad, but a more profound war was being fought at home. Ella was clear about which side of the divide she was on and walked out of the convention in protest of the tactics employed by the Chicago police.

While steadfast in her principles, Ella was by no means an ideologue. She was pragmatic and was not only willing to listen to the views of her opponents but also took them to heart. While she was opposed to the war in Vietnam, she was also sensitive to her conservative working-class constituents who supported it and to the many men from Connecticut's mill towns who served and all too often lost their lives in the conflict. When she ran for the U.S. House of Representatives from the Sixth Congressional District, she kept her distance from the strident rhetoric of the left. She won her seat easily and was reelected for a second term in 1972. She served on the House Education and Labor Committee, championing social programs and labor causes, but she also served on the House Veterans Affairs Committee and concerned herself with the woefully inadequate services and dreadfully unfair treatment that Vietnam veterans faced when they returned home.

Washington, D.C., was no place for Ella, and she quickly grew unhappy there. Now past the age fifty, she saw no chance for gaining influence in the halls of Congress. She saw no effective role for herself apart from that of "the gadfly," and as a doer and not a talker, she had no interest in that sort of grandstanding. At the end of her second term, she longed to return to

Connecticut, and hoping to make a positive difference in the lives of her Nutmeggers, she set her sights on the office of governor.

Running for the office of Connecticut's chief executive, Ella Grasso became more of a "traditionalist," placing herself in the center of the political spectrum. The move was not the typical triangulation of a cynical politician but rather motivated by a genuine desire to serve all the people of the state. While maintaining a progressive stance on social issues, she also supported conservative causes, such as opposing the implementation of a state sales tax. She supported the integration of public schools but opposed busing as an ineffective and unnecessarily disruptive method of doing so. She respected the Supreme Court decision of *Roe v. Wade* as "the law of the land," which she vowed to uphold, but still made clear that, as a devout Catholic, she was morally opposed to abortion. She supported social services and housing for the poor, elderly and mentally disabled but promised to bring her own personal traits of common sense and frugality to bear on the governing of the state and made clear that she would constrain the state's explosive growth in spending. Ella won the 1974 election easily, and on January 8, 1975, she made history by becoming the eighty-third governor of Connecticut.

Old Lyme celebrated Ella's election by declaring "Ella Day" and immediately drew up a bipartisan committee to "honor her election and recognize her leadership." When Ella arrived for the celebration at Old Lyme's Center School, she wasn't immediately recognized and was nearly kicked out of the governor's reserved parking spot. Rather than riding in a conventional limousine or luxury car, Ella drove up in a plain and economical blue sedan. Never one for flash or ostentation, she didn't arrive with a large staff of flunkies and bevy of photographers. She showed up with one assistant, and to most people, she looked like an ordinary citizen. Soon, the rest of the state would come to know and love Ella's natural, down-to-earth style.

It was a style that not only served her well but was also necessary for the times. In the weeks after her inauguration, Ella discovered that the state was in dire fiscal condition, and the budget deficit was far worse than anyone had thought or reported. While she promised to bolster social programs, it became clear to her that setting the state's fiscal house in order was her first priority if she were to accomplish anything further as governor. She made some unpopular moves, slashing programs and laying off state workers. While many of her liberal supporters were dismayed, others were cheered that she didn't spare her own office when swinging the budget axe. She sold the state

Governor Ella Grasso greets Center School students at Ella Day, January 18, 1975. *Ella Day, Town of Old Lyme.*

limo and airplane that had been used by her predecessors and instead got around in a regular police car. She turned off the lights on the capitol dome and cut her own salary. In this way, she conveyed her Depression-era values that while times may be tough, we are all in it together.

By the end of her first term, she had set the state back on a firm fiscal footing, and the large budget deficits had turned to surpluses. She accomplished this through deep budget cuts and hikes in the state sales tax, but she avoided the implementation of the highly unpopular notion of a state income tax. Though raising the regressive sales tax and eschewing the progressive income tax further alienated her liberal base, by setting the state's fiscal house in order, she was soon able to reinstate and expand public health, education, housing and welfare programs. She also made unprecedented investments in innovative programs helping the elderly and mentally disabled.

While her first term was a success, her reelection in 1978 was not a sure thing as she had alienated so many of her traditional supporters early in her administration. There was an event in February of that year that would not only change the dynamic of that election but also forever define the character of Ella Grasso for many of Connecticut's citizens. For better or for worse, natural disasters often determine a politician's legacy. For Ella, her masterful response to the blizzard of 1978 immortalized her reputation as an effective leader, dedicated public servant and no-nonsense do-it-yourself Connecticut Yankee.

For days, meteorologists were predicting a nasty nor'easter that could produce blizzard-like conditions. Ella was scheduled to embark on a fact-finding mission to the Middle East, but seeing the forecast, she wisely decided to cancel the trip and remain in Connecticut to direct the state's response to the impending weather event. The residents of Connecticut were used to snowstorms, but this one promised to be different. As the snow started falling, even the meteorologists were surprised at the storm's sudden increase in intensity. Seeing the furious rate of snowfall, Ella decided that she needed to go to the state armory and personally oversee the state's emergency response. Ella rode through the snow in a police car toward the armory, but on Farmington Avenue, the car got stuck in deep drifts. "That's it," said the state trooper, indicating that they would need to turn back. "No, that's not it," said Governor Grasso, who got out of the car and walked alone for over a mile through the blizzard to reach the armory. When she arrived at its door, she looked like a snowman. She remained there for three days, personally directing the effort and even taking a turn driving a plow.

The residents of the state were confident that even though Ella couldn't stop the snow, no one could stop her, and there was no one better to see the state through its challenge. Her popularity soared after the blizzard. Typically, a politician gravitates toward the self-aggrandizing photo-op or the staged media stunt during a natural disaster, while actually keeping safely out of the fray. That wasn't Ella's style. Her hands-on, "give me a shovel" response fit perfectly with her persona as the caring but tough "Mother Ella" who was always looking out for her citizens. She won the election of 1978 in a landslide.

Ella was inaugurated for her second term as governor on January 3, 1979. She was now not only a popular figure in Connecticut, but increasingly, she was an important player on the national stage, often mentioned in connection with a vice presidential nomination or even presidential run. Tragically, however, Ella's second term would be cut short. In April 1980, she was diagnosed with ovarian cancer, and by the end of the year, it was clear that the treatments were not working. Ella had made her reputation as someone who worked harder than everyone else, who stayed when everyone else went home and the next morning was first to arrive at the office. It was what she expected of herself, and it was what she believed the people of Connecticut deserved. But now, acknowledging that she was not up to the task, she submitted her resignation on December 4, 1980. Lieutenant Governor William O'Neill took over. Two months later, on February 5, 1981, Ella died at the age of sixty-one.

Eulogies and tributes poured in from all over the state and nation, but perhaps none were more eloquent or accurate than that of President Jimmy Carter: "Ella Grasso represented all that is good and promising about politics and public service. As one of the most prominent women in the country, she had the great strength, skill, and when

Statue of Ella Grasso at the capitol in Hartford. *Photograph by Raechel Guest.*

required, toughness. At the same time, she was as loving and compassionate a person as I have known. Her devotion to the less fortunate of our society was untiring."

Bibliography

Abbott, Katherine. *Old Paths and Legends of the New England Border*. New York: GP Putnam and Sons, 1907.

Allyn, Adeline Bartlett. *Black Hall Traditions and Reminisces*. Hartford, CT: Case, Lockwood & Brainard, 1908.

Aronson, Julie. *Bessie Potter Vonnoh—Sculptor of Women*. Cincinnati: Cincinnati Art Museum, Ohio University Press, 2008.

Bakke, Mary Sterling. *A Sampler of Lifestyles: Womanhood and Youth in Colonial Lyme*. Lyme, CT: Advocate Press, 1976.

Barker, G. Stuart, ed. *Landmarks of Old Lyme*. Old Lyme, CT: Connecticut, Ladies' Library Association of Old Lyme, 1968.

Bipartisan Committee in Honor of Governor Ella Grasso. *Ella Day*. Town of Old Lyme, 1975.

Campbell, Susan, and Bill Heald. *Connecticut Curiosities*. Guilford, CT: Globe Pequot Press, 2002.

Chandler, Elisabeth Gordon. Papers and Letters. Lyme Academy College of Fine Arts, Elisabeth Gordon Chandler de Gerenday Archive.

Cummings, Hildegard. "Florence Ann Griswold." Florence Griswold Museum.

Dietrick, Barbara A. *The Ancient Town of Lyme*. Lyme, CT: Lyme Tercentenary Inc. 1965.

Early Lee Family of Lyme and East Lyme, Connecticut. East Lyme, CT: East Lyme Historical Society, 2010.

Ella Grasso Foundation. *Ella*. Hartford, CT: Ella Grasso Foundation 1981.

Ellet, Elizabeth, and Lincoln Diamant. *Revolutionary Women in the War for American Independence.* Westport, CT: Praeger, 1848. Revised and annotated, 1998.

Female Reading Society. *Constitution, Record of Meetings and Membership.* Lyme Historical Society Archive, 1816.

Fenelly, Catherine. *Connecticut Women in the Revolutionary Era.* Chester, CT: Pequot Press, 1975.

Florence Griswold Museum. *Old Lyme: The American Barbizon.* Exhibition catalogue, 1982.

Gardiner, Sarah Diodati. *Early Memories of Gardiner's Island.* East Hampton, NY: East Hampton Star Press, 1947.

Griswold, Wick. *Griswold Point.* Charleston, SC: The History Press, 2014

Hamilton, Alice. *Exploring the Dangerous Trades.* Boston: Little, Brown, and Co., 1943.

Harding, James Ely. *Lyme as It Was and Is.* Lyme, CT: Lyme Bicentennial Commission, 1976.

Hartford and Its Points of Interest. Hartford, CT: Mercantile Illustrating Co., 1895.

Heming, Arthur. *Miss Florence and the Artists of Old Lyme.* Lyme, CT: Lyme Historical Society/Florence Griswold Museum Association, 1971. Reprinted, 2013.

Howard, Daniel. *Connecticut History.* N.p.: privately printed, 1920.

James, May Hall. *An Educational History of Old Lyme, Connecticut 1635–1935.* New Haven, CT: Yale University Press, 1939.

Lee, Irving Call. *The Lee Family.* N.p.: privately printed, 1933.

Little, J. David. *Revolutionary Lyme, A Portrait 1765–1783.* Town of Old Lyme, 1975.

Ludington, Arthur C. *Letters Written From England August 4–November 14, 1914.* N.p.: privately printed.

Ludington, Ethel Saltus, and Louis E. De Forest, eds. *Ludington-Saltus Records.* N.p.: privately printed, 1925.

Ludington, Katharine. *Lyme and Our Family.* N.p.: privately printed, 1928.

Lyme: A Chapter of American Genealogy. Old Lyme, CT: Old Lyme Bicentennial Commission, 1976

MacCurdy Family Papers, circa 1876–1894. Connecticut Historical Society Library.

MacCurdy Family Papers. Old Lyme Historical Society Archive.

MacCurdy-Salisbury Educational Foundation. *Evelyn MacCurdy and the Foundation She Founded.* Old Lyme, CT: privately printed, 1984.

————. *One Century Strong and Growing: 1893–1993*. Old Lyme, CT: privately printed, 1993

Miller, Kristie. *Ellen & Edith—Woodrow Wilson's First Ladies*. Lawrence: University Press of Kansas, 2010.

Morris Museum. *Ellen Axson Wilson and Her Circle*. Exhibition catalogue. Augusta, GA, 2013.

New England Historical and Genealogical Register, January 1918.

Noyes, Charles P. *The Noyes-Gilman Ancestry*. New York: Gilliss Press, 1907.

Noyes Family Papers. Lyme Historical Society. Florence Griswold Museum.

Phoebe Griffin Noyes Library Association. Proceedings at the Opening of the Phoebe Griffin Noyes Library. Old Lyme, CT, 1898.

Purmont, Jon E. *Ella Grasso: Connecticut's Pioneering Governor*. Middletown, CT: Wesleyan University, 2012.

Ritchie, David, and Deborah Ritchie. *Connecticut Off the Beaten Path*. 3rd ed. Old Saybrook, CT: Globe Pequot Press, 1998.

Salisbury, Edward Elbridge, and Evelyn MacCurdy Salisbury. *Family Histories and Genealogies*. New Haven, CT: privately printed, 1892.

Sicherman, Barbara. *Alice Hamilton: A Life in Letters*. Cambridge, MA: Harvard University Press, 1984.

Spring, Joyce. *Daring Lady Flyers*. Nova Scotia, Canada: Pottersfield Press, 1994.

Stark, Bruce P. *Lyme Connecticut: From Founding to Independence*. N.p.: privately printed, 1976.

Stevens, Thomas A. *Old Lyme: A Town Inexorably Linked to the Sea*. Deep River, CT: Deep River Savings Bank, 1959.

Tatum, Alma Merry. *Chronology of the Old Lyme Phoebe Griffin Noyes Library*. Lyme, CT: Friends of the Library, 1988.

————. *For the Love of Books*. Essex, CT: Friends of the Library, OLPGN Library, Hull Press, 1997.

U.S. federal census data for the years 1870–1940.

Willauer, George J. ed. *A Lyme Miscellany 1776–1976*. Middletown, CT: Wesleyan University, 1976.

Wilson, Woodrow. *Papers*, vol. 19, p. 308.

Wolff, Geoffrey. *Black Sun*. New York: Random House, 1976.

NEWSPAPER AND MAGAZINE ARCHIVES

Brooklyn Daily Eagle
Flying magazine
Gazette (Old Lyme)
Hartford Courant
Lewiston Daily Sun
Montreal Gazette
New England Historical and Genealogical Register
New Era (Deep River)
New London Day
New York Newsday
New York Times
Sound Breeze (Old Lyme)
Westfield Leader

FILMS/VIDEOS

In a Nutshell. Directed and produced by Don Bernier. Mimetic Media, 2005.
Once Upon a Time in Old Lyme: The Story of an American Art Colony. Florence Griswold Museum.

ADDITIONAL WEBSITES

Andersen, Jeffrey. "Woodrow and Ellen Wilson in Old Lyme." Online exhibition text. FlorenceGriswoldMuseum.org.
"A Circle of Friends: The Artists of the Florence Griswold House." TFAOI.org.
Chandler, Elisabeth Gordon. "The Lyme Academy Story." TFAOI.org.
CooleyGallery.com.
Ken-Lab History/Bios. Ken-Lab.com.
Metropolitan Museum of Art, New York. *A Young Mother,* by Bessie Potter Vonnoh (object description and Heilebrunn Timeline of Art). www.metmuseum.org.
National First Ladies' Library. Biography of Ellen A. Wilson. firstladies.org.
NewEnglandHistoricalSociety.com.

Wakeman, Carolyn, Caroline Fraser Zinsser, et al. History blog. FlorenceGriswoldMuseum.org.

INTERVIEWS, EMAILS, PERSONAL SOURCES

Diana Atwood-Johnson
C. Townsend Ludington
Amy Roper
Shirley Talcott
Whitney Talcott

Index

About the Authors

Michaelle Pearson holds a bachelor of arts in journalism and photography from Creighton University and a juris doctor from New York Law School. She was director of copy at Arnell Group and continues to work as a freelance writer and editor. Michaelle is a member of the Old Lyme Phoebe Griffin Noyes Library Board, a trustee of the Old Lyme Historical Society and a member of the New York Genealogical & Biographical Society and the Connecticut Society of Genealogists. She is the chief writer/ editor of *River & Sound*, the Old Lyme Historical Society newsletter, and was honored with the society's Chairman's Award in 2013.

Jim Lampos and Michaelle Pearson on Lyme Street, 2013. Angela Chicoski Photography.

Jim Lampos received his bachelor of arts in sociology (*summa cum laude*) from Brandeis University, where he was inducted into Phi Beta Kappa. He completed the general course at the London School of Economics and was awarded a Kaplan Fellowship to attend the New School for Social Research, where he received his master of arts in urban affairs and policy analysis. Jim is a published poet and musician who has released seven CDs, toured nationally and been featured on network television. In 2010, he and his wife, Michaelle Pearson, wrote a history of Old Lyme's beach communities entitled *Rumrunners, Governors, Beachcombers and Socialists*, published by the Old Lyme Historical Society.